Design of Road Drainage System

A Design cum Reference Book

S.N. Sachdeva

Design of Road Drainage System

A Design cum Reference Book

First Edition

Published: June 10, 2018

Createspace, an Amazon company

ISBN-10: 1727735021

ISBN-13: 978-1727735024

DEDICATION

To my beloved daughter Saumya
and
my respected father Sh. Chaman Lal Sachdeva
for inspiring me
from their Heavenly Abode

CONTENTS

ACKNOWLEDGMENTS

My acknowledgements to:

Er. **Harish Gandhi**, formerly M. Tech research scholar, N.I.T. Kurukshetra, Haryana, India for help in bringing the subject matter of the book to the level of publishing.

My children Harshit and Hardik, my wife Dr. Mamta for their warmth and care, my mother Mrs Kailsh Vanti for her blessings, my family and friends for their support .

The almighty God for enabling me in all respects.

1 INTRODUCTION

1.1 GENERAL

Proper drainage system is one of the basic requirements of a road project. Any deficiency in the road drainage system can lead to premature failure of pavement besides causing serious traffic management problems. Poorly drained roads are not only susceptive to reduce the traffic capacity but are also a traffic hazard to the users. Poor drainage increases maintenance/rehabilitation cost of roads, whereas efficient drainage system enhances life of pavements, provides facility for free flow of traffic, substantially reduces life cycle costs, results in better performance of roads and appreciation from road users.

Drainage system can be divided into two main parts viz. surface and subsurface drainage. Adequate arrangements to cater for both surface as well as subsurface drainage are essential to prevent flooding of roads, weakening of road structure, formation of potholes and striping of bitumen. The aim of good design should, therefore, be to remove the surface water efficiently and to keep water table /standing water by the road side well below the pavement. Pavements are damaged more by water than from the effect of large volume of traffic. It is a well-known fact that the rate of serviceability loss of pavement in case of saturated subgrades is much higher as compared to those on dry sub grade soils.

The performance of road drainage in case of urban areas, where roads are usually in flat terrain, is also dependent on the existing drainage system of the area and the same has to be evolved keeping in view the site constraints. Generally main drainage system in urban areas becomes inadequate much before the design life due to urbanization of area and/or increased construction activities and cannot be augmented due to either the problem in acquisition of additional land or availability of funds. As the maintenance of main drainage system rests with local municipalities, the road authorities have no or a very little say in the matter.

Though every local authority has norms for proper maintenance of the drainage system, the same are seldom adhered to in practice due to either constraints of funds or lack of importance assigned by the staff. All these factors results in choking of main drains and failure/non-performance of the drainage system. The main drains in urban areas are generally used as dumping places for garbage, road sweepings, plastic materials and other waste materials which reduce the capacity resulting in practically non performance of the drainage system.

The poor maintenance of the main drainage system adds to the problem of draining of surface water leading to failure of even well designed pavement and drainage system of the road.

To overcome this problem, the practice in advanced countries, is to install sufficient number of garbage collection bins at convenient places in urban areas and there are laws to impose heavy fine for dumping waste material at any other place. The system works well and helps indirectly in performance of drainage system to its maximum capacity.

In addition to peculiar problems in urban areas, there are some locations that pose special problems. Flyover approaches and valley curves require special arrangements for drainage including proper pumping system. The problem of poor drainage is also noticed on diversion roads during execution of improvement works, underpasses, rotaries and multilane intersections where even normal rain results pools of water causing frequent traffic jams, breakdown of vehicles or skidding of vehicles.

It is essential that existing drainage system in construction areas is reviewed and augmented before taking up any improvement work. During execution of a road construction project, draining characteristics of the area in vicinity are charged due to excavation/dumping of materials, but augmentation or modifications in the existing arrangements like correction in camber arrangements for efficient drainage of water from depressions, provision of additional side drains/pipes, frequent clearance of drainage channel etc. are never carried out. Adequacy of drainage of existing pavement/diversion roads is also not investigated for changed conditions/ concentration of traffic. Apart from pavement, the shoulders/berms are also not dressed to match with the slope of carriageway resulting in longitudinal flow of water along the road and side drains are rendered as nonperforming.

The importance of road drainage system in the book is highlighted with the results of a study that was taken up in Panipat, an industrial city of

Haryana, India. The study results show the issues involved with the present drainage system of roads in a typical Indian city. It also exhibits the urgent need for a rational design of road drainage system.

1.2 PANIPAT CITY: A BACKGROUND

1.2.1 Haryana

Haryana is a small state in North India. It has a total of 81 cities and towns. It has 6759 villages. There are 22 districts. Haryana is situated in the North between 27°37' to 30°35' latitude and between 74°28' to 77°36' longitude. Haryana has UP on its Eastern border, Punjab on the Western boarder; Uttranchal, H.P. and Shivalik Hills on its Northern border and Delhi, Rajasthan and Aravali hills on its Southern border. The altitude of Haryana varies between 213 m to 274 m above the mean sea level. An area of 3.5% is covered by forests. Haryana has four main geographical features.

(i)   Shivalik Hills: Their altitude varies between 900m to 2300m. These hills are the source of the rivers like Saraswati, Ghaggar, Tangri and Markanda. These are spread over parts of Panchkula, Ambala and Yamuna Nagar districts.

(ii) Ghaggar Yamuna Plain: It is divided in two parts – the higher one is called "Bangar" and the lower "Khadar". This alluvium plain is made up of sand clay and silt and hard calcareous balls like gravel known locally as kankar.

(iii) Semi desert sandy plain: This area includes the districts of Sirsa and parts of Hissar, Mahendergarh, Fatehabad, Bhiwani and shares border with Rajasthan.

(iv) Aravali Hills: This is a dry irregular hilly area covering parts of South Haryana such as Rewari, Tosham and Gurgaon.

The main transport systems in Haryana are Roads and Railways. Haryana has more than 30,000 km. of paved roads, making it one of the most well connected states in whole of Asia. Every village of the state is now linked with paved roads. The length of the National Highways passing through Haryana is more than 2000 km. Out of many National Highways that pass through Haryana, some of the important NHs are:

NH-1   Delhi-Panipat-Karnal-Ambala-Amritsar (S.S.S. Marg or G.T. Road)

NH - 2   Delhi – Faridabad – Agra – Mathura – Kolkata (S.S.S. Marg
            or G.T. Road)
NH - 8   Delhi – Gurgaon – Jaipur – Mumbai
NH - 10   Delhi – Rohtak – Hissar – Sirsa – Fazilka
NH - 21   Chandigarh – Manali
NH - 22   Ambala – Zirakpur – Kalka – Shimla – Shipakila

Recently, the Govt of India has issued the revised nomenclature for these NHs and their numbers are changed like NH-1 has become NH-44. However, still these NHs are known mostly by their old numbers.

The state has about 3135 km State Highways, 7687 km Major District Roads and about 17190 km Rural and other roads.

Water is available in plenty as Haryana is a land of canals. The annual rainfall in the state is about 455mm. About 70% rainfall is received during the month of July to September and the remaining rainfall is received during December to February.

The underground water resources differ from area to area. The depth of water-table is the lowest in the Khadar area along the Yamuna, where it is below 3m. It increases to 13 to 17m and even higher in some of the western and south-eastern parts of the state. The ground water is mostly used for drinking purposes as well as for industrial, irrigation and other uses.

Irrigation of the state depends on the water provided by the canals. The various canals, which are operating in the state include Western Yamuna canal, Gurgaon canal, Jui canal, Jawahar Lal Nehru canal and Bhakra canal. These canals are the main source of water for cultivation in various districts of the state.

1.2.2 Panipat City

Panipat is an ancient and historic city in Panipat District, Haryana state, India. It is located at 90 km from Delhi on National Highway-1 and comes under the National Capital Territory of Delhi. Its Geographical coordinates are 29°23' 20"N and 76°58'5"E. The three sides of Panipat touch other district of Haryana – Karnal in the North, Jind in the West and Sonepat in the South. Panipat borders U.P. across Yamuna in the East. The location of Panipat is shown in Fig. 1.1.

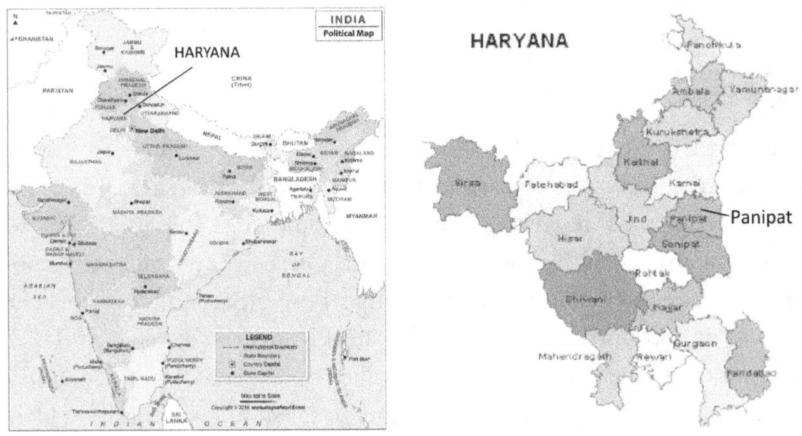

Fig 1.1 Location of Panipat City

Panipat was the part of District Karnal until October 31, 1989. It has an average elevation of 219m (718 feet).

<u>Demographics</u>

As of 2001 India census, Panipat had a population of 9,67,449. Males constitute 55% of the population. Panipat has an average literacy rate of 69%, which is higher than the national average of 59.5%. Male literacy is 73% and female literacy is 64%.

Industries

Panipat is a city of textiles and carpets. It is the biggest centre for cheap blankets and carpets in India and has a handloom weaving industry. The pickle "Pachranga International" is also well known. Panipat also has heavy industry, with an oil refinery of Indian Oil Corporation, the National Fertilizers Limited plant and the Thermal Power Station. It is the biggest centre in the country for producing shoddy (recycled) yarn and a large consumer of rags for reprocessing. It is the biggest centre in the country for producing low priced blankets and a traditional supplier of barrack blankets to the armed forces. The town has infrastructure such as rail, road and inland container depot well suited to industry and export.

Road Network of Panipat

The road network of Panipat includes two National Highways, two State Highways, some district roads and other urban roads coming in and out of the city centre. The main roads of the city are: Panipat-Delhi Road (NH-1), Panipat-Gohana Road (NH-71A), Panipat-Shamli Road (Sanoli Road, SH-16) and Panipat-Assandh-Jind Road (SH-14). The total length of main road network is about 30 km. There is a 3.6 km long six-lane flyover on NH-1 bypassing the through traffic from Panipat. The flyover passes over the central built up section of Panipat city. Two lanes peripheral roads with paved shoulders have been constructed on either side of the flyover to cater to the internal traffic of Panipat.

National Highways passing through the city are under the jurisdiction of National Highway Authority of India whereas State Highways and district roads are under Haryana PWD (B&R). Other roads fall in the jurisdiction of various departments such as Irrigation Branch, Haryana Urban Development Authority, Marketing Board and Municipal Corporation.

Most of the main roads are provided with bituminous pavements. These roads have received significant maintenance over the past decade. The roads constructed in the last few years without proper drainage system are now facing service condition problems. Pavements constructed with proper drainage system show only a few signs of deterioration.

1.3 DRAINAGE PROBLEMS AND DESIGN

Poor drainage results into losses, direct and indirect, in the form of damaged roads and reduced serviceability. In spite of this, adequate priority for drainage system is rarely accorded, whether it is in the matter of planning, design, organization, fund allocation or monitoring. Funds required for a drainage system are small as compared to the development of road infrastructure and the recurring losses, which the society and the Government have to bear from year to year are enormous. It is necessary that due priority is given to the drainage of roads and satisfactory arrangements ensured by way of proper design and planning of drainage system to ensure sustainability of road infrastructure. The book "Design of Road Drainage System" is an attempt towards recognizing the importance of drainage for roads. The book aims at exhibiting the importance of road drainage and proper design of drainage system by an example of a study taken up in one of the cities of India covering the following main aspects:

(i)   Drainage system of Panipat and its main roads.

(ii) Analyses of the drainage related data of main roads of Panipat city.

(iii) Assessment of the adequacy/deficiencies of the existing drainage system.

(iv) Design of drainage system as per provisions of Indian Roads Congress (IRC).

(v)   Co-relations between design parameters for their easy application.

(vi) Guidelines for procedural application of results of the study for determination of design discharge for the design of road side drainage system for roads.

The study has been undertaken on the identified stretches of the following main roads of Panipat city:

- Amritsar-Ambala-Panipat-Delhi Road (NH- 1) : G.T. Road

- Panipat-Gohana-Rohtak Road (NH- 71A) : Gohana Road

- Panipat-Assandh-Jind Road (SH-14) : Assandh Road

- Panipat-Shamli-Meerut Road (SH- 16): Sanoli Road

The drainage related data were collected in respect of these roads for the stretches passing through Panipat city area. All stretches of the roads are located in plain terrain.

The book though is based upon the outcome of a study that was conducted on identified stretches of the above roads; the results may be generalized and used for other such roads having similar roadway and environmental conditions as in the study area.

2   GUIDELINES FOR URBAN DRAINAGE SYSTEM

2.1 GENERAL

The importance of adequate and efficient drainage in the structural integrity of a road is well recognized. A drainage problem is caused by an excess of water either on the surface of the pavement or below the surface of the pavement. Thus the road drainage falls into two distinct categories:

a)   Surface Drainage – to remove water from areas of carriageway or footpath where its presence would be harmful or dangerous to users or lead to deterioration of pavement. The flowing water has the capacity to damage the road while flowing down the shoulders and side slopes. In this process, the water causes erosion and again deposits the material causing siltation at other point, both requiring provision of measures to reduce the damage due to each. If the road profile is not correct and conducive to quick drainage, pools of water may form, weakening the pavement course and leading to skidding, hydroplaning or splashing of water, which is a nuisance to vehicles and may lead to accidents.

b)   Subsoil Drainage – to drain-off the subsoil water sufficiently away from the influence zone of carriageway to sustain the stability of pavement support within design tolerances.
The urban roads usually are in flat terrain. Urbanization of the area and intense density of construction needs well-planned drainage. Roads and highways do not have a distinctly separate drainage system. Water from the road joins the roadside drain through inlets or gratings. For effective drainage, this should join the peripheral drains, which in turn should join the main drain for ultimate discharge to the natural drain. Storm water drainage, thus has to take into account alignments, levels on ground and outfall levels.

In most of the urban areas, responsibility for design and construction of peripheral and trunk drainage system rests with local bodies; e.g. Municipal Corporation; while that of road side drain with the road construction agency like PWD. For an effective system proper coordination between all concerned agencies is a must. The following paragraphs discuss mainly the guidelines of IRC: SP: 50 [1] for urban drainage system.

2.2 GENERAL CRITERIA FOR ROAD DRAINAGE

2.2.1 Minimum Longitudinal Gradient

For better internal drainage of pavement layers, especially of granular material a slight longitudinal gradient is preferable. A minimum longitudinal gradient of 0.3% (about 1 in 333) is adequate for satisfactory drainage.

2.2.2 Pavement Cross Slope / Camber

For quick disposal of precipitation on the road surface, it would be necessary that water has to travel least distance through reasonably steep cross slope. However, from the consideration of comfort to the traffic, steep cross slope is objectionable. As such a judicious balance is required between the two requirements.

For urban roads having divided carriageway, the camber is unidirectional away from the median. In case of super elevated sections, either gap in the central verge with suitable adjustments in the levels of the two carriageways or in extreme cases, central drainage arrangement is resorted to.

When the road is on gradient, the flow is governed by the resultant slope produced by longitudinal and cross slope. In such a case, in order that water travels the least distance on road surface (more the distance more is the quantity of sheet flow causing hydroplanning) the camber should be 0.7 of the longitudinal gradient or the camber values specified in table 2.1 for a particular road surface whichever is higher. In other words, on steep gradients on long length of road, the camber should be increased to get satisfactory drainage conditions.

Special care is also required in detailing the valley curves so that such locations do not collect water.

Table 2.1 Camber Values for Straight Sections

S. No.	Surface Type	Camber/Cross fall
1.	Graveled or WBM surface	2.5-3.0 %
2.	Thin bituminous surfacing	2.0-2.5 %
3.	High type bituminous surfacing or Concrete surfacing	1.7-2.0 %

Note: Higher value of camber should be adopted in areas with high intensity of rainfall and where ponding is expected due to any reason. Steeper camber should also be provided on kerbed pavements to minimize the spread of surface water.

2.2.3 Shoulders and Footpath Drainage

For shoulders along unkerbed pavements the cross-fall should be at least 0.5% steeper than that of the pavement subject to the minimum values given in Table 2.2:

Table 2.2 Crossfall for Shoulders for Unkerbed Pavement

Surface Type	Cross fall
WBM surface	3%
Gravel surface	4%
Earthen surface	5%

In addition, it is necessary that shoulders are not higher than adjoining pavement surface for quick drainage.

For paved footpaths, a cross fall of 3 to 4% should be adopted. For verges and unpaved areas cross falls should be 4 to 6%.

Precipitation from the road surface flows towards outer edge of carriageway (except where central drainage arrangement has been provided) into kerb channel where kerb and footpaths are provided. The kerb channel should be 30 cm wide with smooth finish and should have a minimum transverse slope of 1 in 6. The longitudinal slope of kerb channel is guided by the road gradient. In reaches where there is no longitudinal gradient in the road, kerb channel should slope towards kerb inlets or bell mouths. The kerb channel discharges its flow into pipes through bell mouth (named after its shape) which should be 300mm dia non- pressure RCC pipes placed under footpath at about 10-15m interval. These pipes discharge into roadside drain.

2.2.4 Median Drainage

In urban areas, medians are usually less than 5m width and kerbed except in cases where wider medians are provided as part of future widening. As such medians should be crowned wherever paved or turfed for drainage across the pavement. Care should be taken that earth surface in the median are not sloped to drain on the road as washed away soil may deposit on road pavement making it slippery and accident prone. Earth in median should be 2.5 cm below the kerb.

In locations where carriageway is sloping towards the median, as may be the case where road is in curvature, there are two alternatives for the disposal of rain water.

(i)   The rainwater is collected in the median drain through inlets at suitable intervals. At intervals rainwater could be removed from the median through a drain or pipe across the carriageway to roadside drain.

(ii) Water is collected in the manholes within the median provided at a distance of about 15 m by giving a longitudinal slope in the channel on either side of the manhole. The water collected in the manhole is then taken to the main drain on the side of the road through a 450 mm dia RCC pipe across the carriageway on any one side depending upon the site condition. The cover on the pipe should be at least 300 mm.

2.2.5 Drainage of High Embankment

In high embankments and approaches to bridges/over bridges, if the water is allowed to leave the carriageway at undefined spots, it may cause serious damages to the embankment and eventually undermine the pavement. In each location, rainwater is collected in small manageable quantities through longitudinal kerb channel and brought down through chutes without damage. The chutes may be lined with cement concrete on stable supports and may be located at 10 to 15 m intervals depending upon the rainfall and width of carriageway.

2.2.6   Longitudinal Gradient

The minimum longitudinal gradient is governed by drainage consideration. On unkerbed pavements, near level longitudinal gradients may not be objectionable when the pavement has sufficient cross fall/camber to drain rain water laterally. But for better internal drainage in pavement layers especially of granular material, a slight longitudinal gradient is preferable. Also in cut sections and medians a longitudinal gradient of 0.3 % (1 in 333) is considered desirable in most conditions to secure satisfactory removal of water.

A minimum longitudinal gradient of 0.3 % is also preferable to facilitate flow of water in side drains; with outlets provided at required interval to restrict the depth of drains.

2.3 STORM WATER DRAINAGE DESIGN

The design of the drainage system involves (i) calculating the total discharge that the system will require to drain off and (ii) fixing the slope and dimensions of the drain to have adequate capacity to carry the discharge and afford proper maintenance. These two aspects are dealt separately in the following paragraphs.

The discharge is dependent upon intensity and duration of precipitation characteristics of the area and the time required for such flow to reach the drain. The storm water flow for this purpose may be determined by various methods like rational method, hydrograph method, rainfall run off estimation, correlation studies, digital computer models and empirical formulae.

The empirical formulae that are available for estimating the storm water runoff can be used only when comparable conditions to those for which the equations are derived initially can be assured. Of the different methods available the rational formula is most commonly used and serves the purpose for design of road side drains satisfactorily.

Any method requires that existing rainfall data of the concerned area is analyzed to permit a suitable forecast. Roadside drains are not designed for the peak flow of rare occurrences such as once in 100 years or 50 years. However, it is necessary to provide sufficient capacity to prevent too frequent a flooding of the drainage area. There may be some water accumulations on the roads when the rainfall exceeds the design value, which has to be permitted. The frequency of occurrence, which can be permitted, varies from place to place, depending upon the importance of the place and expectancy of the public. Flooding at any time, however, causes inconvenience to people but they may accept it once in a while considering the savings affected in drainage cost. Based on the practice being followed in metropolitan cities in our country and cost consideration in mind, it is recommended that a return period of one to two years be adopted for urban roads in estimation of run-off. For higher category roads, like N.Hs, a higher return period may be adopted.

2.3.1 Time of concentration

It is the time required for the maximum run-off rate to develop. It is equal to the time required for a drop of water to run from the most remote point of the road surface to the point for which the run-off is being estimated. Empirical formula (2.1) may be used to determine the time of concentration.

$$t_c = (0.87 \times L^3 / H) \times 0.385 \tag{2.1}$$

Where

t_c = time of concentration in hours

L = distance of critical point to the drain in km

H = fall in level from the critical point to the drain level in meters

The formula described above can be used for each storm line to the outlet for arriving at the time of concentration.

2.3.2 Intensity of Rainfall

It has been observed that shorter the duration of critical rainfall, the greater would be the expected average intensity during that period. For example during a 30 minutes rainfall, some 5 minutes period, or any period less than 30 minutes in length, will have average rainfall intensity greater than that of the whole storm. The critical duration of rainfall will be which produces maximum runoff. This duration is equal to the time of concentration since shorter periods do not allow the whole area to contribute water and longer duration will give smaller average rainfall intensity. The problem, thus, reduces to one of establishing a relationship between time of rainfall duration and probable or expected rainfall intensity. For the design purpose, high intensities are of importance.

Intensities to be expected vary in different parts of the country. Though the rainfall gauges installed by the meteorological department and other Govt. organization are not numerous enough to give entirely satisfactory data, but sufficient information is available to allow adoption of rain fall intensity. In case of ordinary rain gauge locations, the data available is in terms of daily rainfall i.e. highest one day station rain fall (24 hours rainfall along with date of occurrence).

In locations where only 24-hour rainfall data is available, the same can be converted into short duration rainfall by adopting conversion factors. Alternately, one-hour duration storm intensity may be converted into any duration intensity using the formula (2.2) given by IRC-SP-13 [2].

$$i = [F (T + 1)] / [T (t + 1)] \qquad (2.2)$$

Where

i = intensity of rainfall within a shorter period of 't' hours within a storm

F = total rainfall in a storm in cm falling in duration of storm of T hours

t = smaller time interval in hours within the storm duration of T hours

It is also added that as per practice being followed in most of the metropolitan cities, the calculation of runoff is being carried out using hourly rainfall intensity for a return period of one to two years. This is primarily for simplicity of calculations. However, for a large drainage system, it is recommended that calculations be carried out on the basis of detailed analysis as the efforts may be worth the savings in cost.

2.3.3 Rational Formula for Estimating Peak Run-Off Rates

For small watersheds not exceeding 50 km², as is the usual case for urban drainage system, the rational method is widely used for estimating the peak run of rates. The rational formula is given by equation (2.3).

$$Q \quad = 0.028 \, PAIc \qquad (2.3)$$

Where

Q   = design peak run off in cum/sec

P   = coefficient of run off for catchments characteristics

A   = area of catchment in hectares

Ic   = critical intensity of rainfall in cm/hour for the selected frequency and duration of storm. Duration of storm is equal to time of concentration.

The coefficient of runoff (P) is the portion of precipitation that makes its way to the drain. Its value depends on a large number of factors such as permeability of the surface, type of ground cover, shape and size of catchment area, the topography, the geology, initial state of wetness and duration of storm. The value of 'P' commonly adopted for use in rational formula is given in table 2.3

Table 2.3 Value of Coefficient of Runoff

S. No.	Description of Surface	Coefficient of Run off (P)
1	Watertight pavement surface (concrete or bitumen), steep bare rock	0.90
2	Green area (Loamy)	0.30.
3	Green area (Sandy)	0.20
4	Alluvial area along roads	0.30
5	Lawns and parks	0.15
6	Flat built up area with about 60% area impervious	0.55
7	Moderately steep built up area with 70% area impervious	0.80

2.3.4 Hydraulic Design

(i)   Design of Drain Section

Capacity of the drain is normally designed using Manning's equation (2.4).

$$V = (1/n)\, R^{2/3}\, S^{1/2} \tag{2.4}$$

and then using equation (2.5) to calculate the discharge.

$$Q = A \times V \tag{2.5}$$

Where

Q   =   discharge in cum/sec
V   =   mean velocity in m/sec
n   =   Manning's rugosity coefficient
R   =   hydraulic mean radius which is area of flow cross section divided by wetted perimeter
S   =   gradient of drain bed
A   =   area of flow cross section in m^2

(ii)   Coefficients of Rugosity for various surfaces are indicated in table 2.4.

Table 2.4 Coefficient of Rugosity (n) for Type of Surfaces [1]

S. No.	Type of surface	Value of n
i)	Brick pitched drain	0.017
ii)	Plastered brick surface	0.015
iii)	Plastered brick surface with neat cement finish	0.013
iv)	Concrete pipes upto 600mm dia	0.015
v)	Concrete pipes above 600mm dia	0.013
vi)	Dry. Rubble masonry	0.033
vii)	Dressed ashlar surface	0.015
viii)	Dry. Stone pitching	0.020
ix)	Katcha Drain	0.025

(iii)   <u>While deciding the drain sections</u>, it is not sufficient that they are adequate to carry the required discharge. Following guidelines are also required to be kept in view. Table 2.5 gives minimum and maximum velocities. Table 2.6 depicts minimum free board to be adopted.

Table 2.5 Minimum and Maximum Velocities [1]

S.No.	Type of Drain	Min. Velocity (m/sec)	Max. Velocity (m/sec)
(i)	Internal drain (brick pitched or plastered)	0.45	1.5.
(ii)	Intercepting and main drain (brick pitched or plastered)	0.75	1.5
(iii)	Pipe drain (running full)	0.75	1.8

To ensure self-cleaning of the drain, a minimum velocity of 1.5m per second may be desirable.

Table 2.6 Minimum Free Board [1]

S.No.	Drain size	Free board
i)	Upto 300 mm bed width	10 cm
ii)	Beyond 300 mm and upto 900 mm bed width	15 cm
iii)	Beyond 900 mm and up to 1500 mm bed width	30 cm

For larger drains the free board shall be higher upto 90 cm depending upon the discharge.

(iv)   Minimum Section of Drain

It should be possible to clean the drains periodically using a spade. Accordingly, it is recommended that minimum width of a drain should not be less than 250 mm. In case of pipes the minimum diameter should not be less than 450 mm.

(v)   The effective section of the drain carrying design discharge should be considered below the bell month pipe so that there is no back flow of water on to the road.

2.3.5 Channel Shapes

The usual channel shapes are
(i)   Parabolic
(ii)   Trapezoidal
(iii)   Rectangular
(iv)   Triangular or V-shaped

The parabolic profile is considered to be the best for hydraulic flow but its actual construction and maintenance is difficult. The V-shaped drain is not very popular in urban areas as its desilting is difficult. The trapezoidal and rectangular sections are easy to construct and are considered most suitable.

In urban areas, all drains passing through built up area and near to bus stand, crossing etc. should preferably be covered so that the drains are not used as dustbins.

2.3.6 Economical Sections (For Lined Drains)

As for as possible, for obtaining economical sections the relation between bed width (b) and depth (d) shall be as follows:

(i)   Rectangular drain   b   =   2d
(ii)   Trapezoidal   b   =   0.82 d (1.1 side slope)
                    =   1.24d ($\frac{1}{2}$: 1 side slope)

For main or trunk drains the side slopes should be 1:1 or $\frac{1}{2}$: 1 depending upon nature of soil and availability of land.

2.4   DRAINAGE SYSTEM AND APPURTENANCES

The rainwater from the right of way of the road is ultimately required to be transported away before it can cause damage. The water can be transported away in any of the following manner.

a)   Over the surface

b)   In open channels

c)   In covered drains or pipes

<u>Drainage over surface</u>

All surface water is initially drained over the surface before it is collected in the drainage system. The drains are located along roadside and the water is let into the drain through gulleys, bell mouth or other such water entrances

Minor roads in residential areas are narrow and it may be difficult to provide separate space for drains. In such cases the water can be allowed to flow in the kerb channel, which can be led into the main drainage system where the minor street meets the main road.

<u>Drainage through open channel</u>

The open drains along the road side definitely have to be away from the shoulders or the berm and require additional space. They are easier to maintain and allow removal of silt and other solids easily.

<u>Covered drains or pipe</u>

Covered drains i.e. rectangular drains with cover slabs are free from garbage dumping problems. Also, they can be allocated below the footpath or in extreme cases below the carriageway where space is restricted. The closed system in many cases is demanded by the residents of the adjoining areas.

<u>Selecting</u> the type of drain, cost should not be the only consideration. Cost of maintaining the system and requirement of the area should also be considered. For effective drainage and facility of inspection and maintenance, it is desirable to have open drains. Fencing or boundary wall maybe considered to guard against throwing of garbage and to avoid accidents. Access to houses should be provided by means of properly designed slabs / covers whenever situation so warrants. Such access, if provided by the residents, more often creates a hindrance to the free flow. However, keeping in view other limitations of availability of land in urban

areas, possibility of ingress of garbage and risk to the population living near the drain, it may be necessary to have covered drains. For the purpose of desilting removable slabs, preferably cast under controlled condition for durability, should be provided.

2.4.1 General Considerations in Design of Storm Water Drain

(a)   Drains should be planned taking into consideration the ground levels, slope of the ground, valley and ridges and also the land uses planned for urban development.

(b)   Drains should be planned to get good longitudinal slope, considering the nature of soil and subsoil water level. Aim should be to get a high velocity for the dominant flow.

(c)   Efficiency in maintenance of drainage system should be an important consideration in selecting the size, (covered or open) shape and the location.

(d)   An attempt should be made in the design to provide higher starting and higher outfall bed levels in drains. A free outfall shall be attempted as far as possible.

(e)   Design of the main drain shall be so made as to allow use of the normal devices for desilting operations.

2.4.2 Manholes

<u>Ordinary Manholes</u>: A manhole is an opening constructed on the alignment of a covered or pipe drain for facilitating a person access to it for the purpose of inspection, testing, cleaning and removal of obstruction from the drain.

<u>Spacing</u>: The spacing of manholes depends upon the nature of the drain and the cleaning device likely to be used. Generally, manholes in straight reaches are in the spacing of 10 to 20 m.

<u>Cover and Frame</u>: Pre-cast concrete manhole covers and frames are preferable compared to cast iron covers and frames as these are less prone to theft.

<u>Gratings and curb inlets</u>: These are devices meant to admit the surface run-off to the drain and form a very important part of the system. Storm water inlets may be categorized under three major groups: kerb inlets, gutter inlets and combination inlets.

<u>Kerb inlets</u>

These are the vertical opening in the road kerbs through which the storm water flows and preferred where heavy traffic is anticipated.

<u>Gutter Inlets</u>

These consist of horizontal opening in the drain which is covered by one or more grating through which the flow passes.

<u>Combination Inlets</u>

In some locations, due to vertical or horizontal space restrictions, combination of the two may be adopted to act as a single unit.

<u>Bell Mouth Inlets</u>

In urban areas, where footpath is made and the location of the drain is adjacent to it, water inlet in many cases is through an RCC pipe. This is 250 mm dia pipe. The schematic arrangement is shown in fig 2.1.

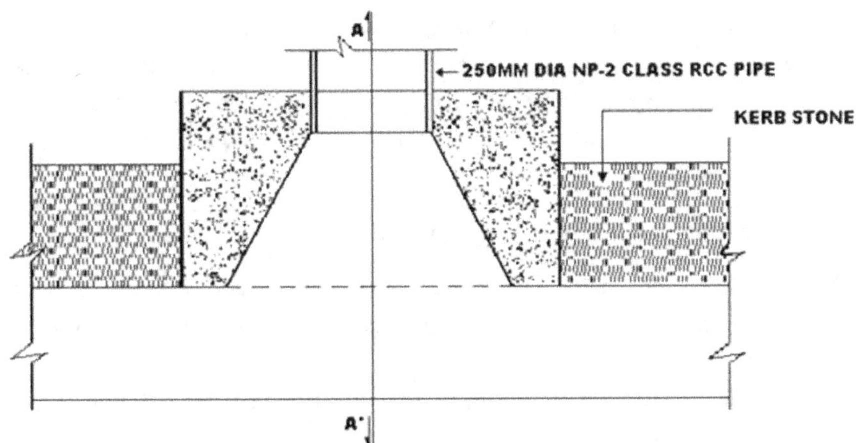

Fig. 2.1 Schematic arrangement showing Bell-Mouth drain

2.5 SUB SURFACE DRAINAGE

For design of sub surface drainage system the source and quantum must be determined. The ingress of water may take place from

(a) Top i.e. surface infiltration of rainwater through paved or unpaved area.

(b) Lateral seepage through shoulders and verges, and

(c)   Free water from a high water table or capillary action from a water table.

In most urban areas the percentage of built up surface area is rather high and as such situations with problems of subsurface water may not be frequent unless the water table is unusually high and the subgrade soil is poor from point of view of drainage. Physical condition of nearby roads, presence of vegetation, which usually occurs in wet soils and the local experience, helps in selecting areas for detailed investigation. During detailed investigation following information is collected:

(i)   Rainfall data for the area and the design storm.

(ii) Assessment of grounds water conditions. This is achieved by making boreholes, trenches and pits. Water levels and inflows should be carefully recorded at the time of excavation. Pumping tools can be used to establish the in-situ permeability of materials and the rate of recoupment of ground water.

(iii) Assessment of the soil properties, information in respect of soil classification. Atterberg limits and moisture content of soil at subgrade level and other levels in areas where water is present is collected.

2.5.1 Drainage of Subsurface Infiltration

Road surfaces, medians, shoulders and higher adjoining area are permeable and the precipitation invariably seeps down. Collection of water in potholes and undulations etc also contributes through cracks in pavements particularly due to ageing defects. Joints also permit ingress of water into the roads structure. For design purpose, the quantity of water, which is required to be drained off, is dependent upon the intensity of rainfall and the coefficient of infiltration or the infiltration factor. Commonly adopted ranges are:

(i)   Earthen shoulder   =   0.4 to 0.6
(ii) Bituminous pavements   =   0.2 to 0.4
(iii) Concrete pavement   =   0.3 to 0.4

The best way of drainage of pavement course is to provide and extend a specially designed sub base layer up to the embankment slope face. In urban situations this may not always be possible. In such a case, provision of a sub surface drain is made. The sub base layer and the sub surface drain should have sufficient capacity to carry the design discharges.

Flow through sub base layer, which is considered as saturated laminar flow is calculated using Darcy's law and the flow through pipes is calculated using manning formulae. The Darcy's law is given in equation (2.6).

$$Q = K\,i\,A \tag{2.6}$$

Where

Q = discharge in m^3/sec

K = coefficient of permeability in m/sec

i = hydraulic gradient

A = cross section Area in m^2 perpendicular to the direction of flow

Sub base and base should have self-draining provisions by extending granular drainage layer fully over the road formation width. In addition, proper cross fall to the drainage layer should be provided to guard against any sluggish flow.

As a general rule, the lower payment layer should be more permeable than the upper one. In case of existing pavements, where such situation may become unavoidable from other considerations, the overlaid layer having larger voids should be drained off laterally to avoid interfacial drainage problems and premature failure of the overlaid layer. Typical arrangements of drainage of pavement are shown in Fig. 2.2.

Darcy's law is applicable for sub surface flow of water, however, in actual practice one encounters soil or rock formations, which are highly heterogeneous and have anisotropic permeability. Application of theoretical models to complex natural situations can lead to error in estimation of quantity of flow and flow conditions. For these reasons field observations and measurements are the best guide.

For a successful design using range of permeability for a given material, the highest permeability value should be used when the material is to act as a barrier and the lowest value used when the material is used to allow water to pass through.

Typical arrangement indicating use of deep formation drain is shown in Fig. 2.3.

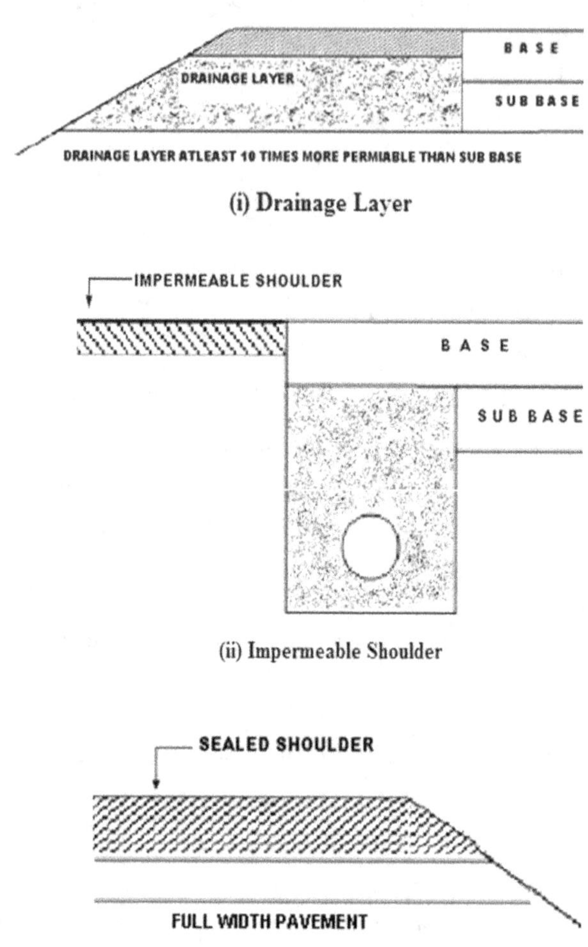

(i) Drainage Layer

(ii) Impermeable Shoulder

(iii) Sealed Shoulder

Fig. 2.2 Examples of satisfactory pavement drainage

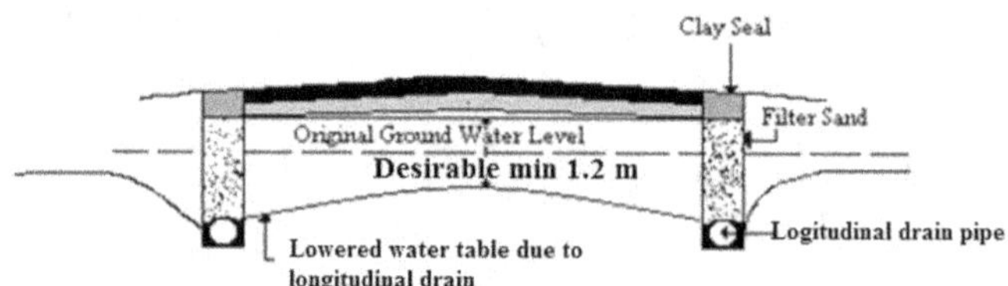

Fig. 2.3 Arrangement of Deep Formation drain

2.5.2 Aggregate Filters

A properly designed and installed aggregate filter should be able to retain soil and prevent soil particle movement, thus eliminating piping potential. Properly designed aggregate filters ensure that there are no large voids within the filter and particularly at the soil filter interface of a sub surface drainage structure.

A single component aggregate filter may be used to protect relatively coarse soils whereas drainage through fine soils usually requires a multi layered aggregate filter. A multilayered filter consists of a fine aggregate gradation which retains the natural soil particles at their original positions and a coarser filter aggregate which prevents particles of the fine aggregate filter from migrating into the perforations of a drainage pipe or granular water transport medium.

MORTH [3] gives the grading requirement for filter material and aggregate drains. These are as given in tables 2.7 and 2.8.

It must be remembered that if the aggregate gradation is too coarse, the gaps and voids at the soil aggregate interface may be so large that the adjacent soil particles will not be retained, However if the gradation is too fine, inefficient water flow may result in build up of hydrostatic pressure.

Table 2.7 Grading requirements for filter material [3]

Sieve Designation (mm)	Percent by weight passing the sieve		
	Class I	Class II	Class III
53	-	-	-
45	-	-	97-100
26.5	-	100	-
22.4	-	95-100	58-100
11.2	100	48-100	20-60
5.6	92-100	28-54	4-32
2.8	83-100	20-35	0-10
1.4	59-96	-	0-5
0.710	35-80	6-18	-
0.355	14-40	2-9	-
0.180	3-15	-	-
0.090	0-5	0-4	0-3

Note: When the soil around the trench is fine grained (fine silt or clay) then class I gradation, when coarse silt to medium sand and sandy soil, then class-II gr. and when gravelly sand then class III grading should be used.

The thickness of back fill material around the pipe should not be less than 150mm. considering minimum ø of the pipe as 150 mm; width of the trench should not be less than 450mm.

Table 2.8 Grading requirements for aggregate drains [3]

Sieve size	Percent passing by weight	
	Type A	Type B
63 mm	-	100
37.5 mm	100	85-100
9.5 mm	-	0-20
3.35 mm	45-100	0-5
600 micron	25-80	-
150 micron	8-45	-
75 micron	0-10	-

2.5.3 Fabric Filters

Filter fabrics or geotextile are generally manufactured from polyethylene or polypropylene or similar fibers either woven or non-woven in variety. Geotextile eliminates the need for aggregate filters. The fine pore size and high permeability of these filters make the filter suitable for protecting a broad range of soil gradations. Some typical examples of use of fabrics as a filter are shown in Fig. 2.4.

2.5.4 Purpose of Subsoil Drainage System

The purpose of the sub soil drainage is to collect the water from its source and ultimately dispose off to a place where it can do no harm to the road. It consists of the filter, the pipe inlets, intermediate pits and the outlet. Marker pegs are also installed to indicate their location. Schematic diagram of the system is shown in fig. 2.5

2.5.5 Use of Subsoil Drainage for Special Locations

In urban area, utility services usually run parallel to the road and in many cases, due to widening of roads they get buried below the pavement or the footpath. Due to large temperature variation particularly when the season changes and vibration of the moving traffic, some of the joints of underground water supply pipes may leak leading to sub soil water conditions and damage to road. In such locations, sub soil water drainage arrangements should be made to safeguard the structural soundness of the road.

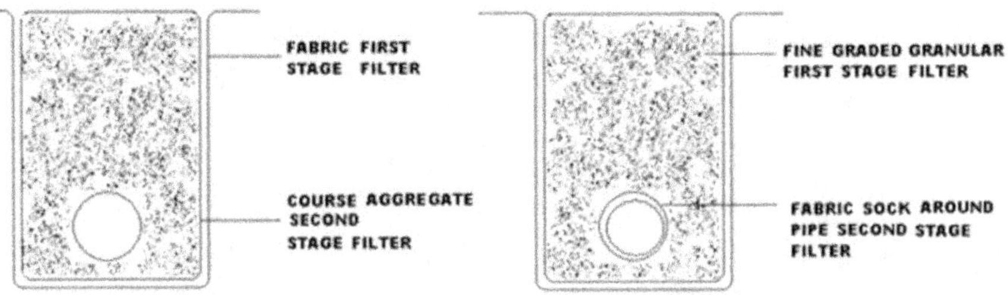

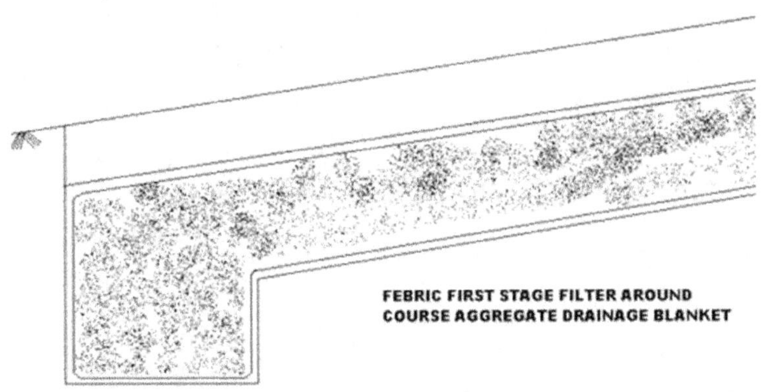

Fig. 2.4 Uses of fabric filters

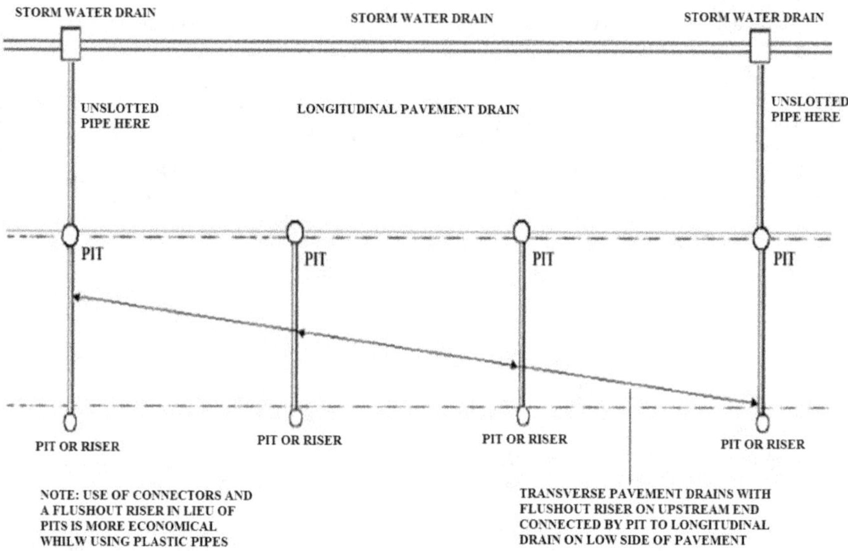

Fig. 2.5 Plan of Sub-soil drainage system

3 DRAINAGE SYSTEM OF PANIPAT CITY

3.1 GENERAL

A preliminary study of the field conditions of the city was made and relevant records of the area were gathered to know the drainage system of the city. The general data related to drainage of the area and road specific data for the selected roads were collected by field studies and from relevant records of the area. Analyses of the data were carried out to understand the drainage system of the area and also to evolve the roadside drainage system for the selected roads.

A preliminary filed study of the area and the study of relevant documents obtained from the concerned departments were taken up to develop an understanding of the drainage system of the study area. The drainage system of Panipat city and its general deficiencies based upon this study are discussed in this chapter. Various aspects related to the drainage system such as wastewater disposal, solid waste management and sewerage system in the area are also discussed.

3.2 PANIPAT DRAIN

The topographic map of Panipat depicted in Fig.3.1 [4] on 1:50000 scale was studied on which the water points crossing the road were identified. The schematic diagram developed from this map showing the roads selected for the study and the drainage system of the city is given in Fig. 3.2. It is observed that there is only one stream, known as Panipat drain (Gandha Nala), through which all the storm water of the city flows. While moving towards Delhi, the stream at start of the city is located on west side of NH-1. It crosses NH-1 from west to east at km 91.400 as shown in Fig. 3.2. It then moves further eastward and then flows parallel to the road up to km 87.000.

The Panipat drain originates from village Kabri. It outfalls in the main drain near village Simla Gujran as shown in Fig. 3.2 and Plate 3.1. Then the discharge of main drain falls in River Yamuna.

The water from the storm water drains is discharged in the Panipat drain as per the following scheme. North of km 89.940 the water is taken parallel to the road in the roadside drain and discharged into the Panipat drain through the bridge at km 91.4 near PWD rest house.

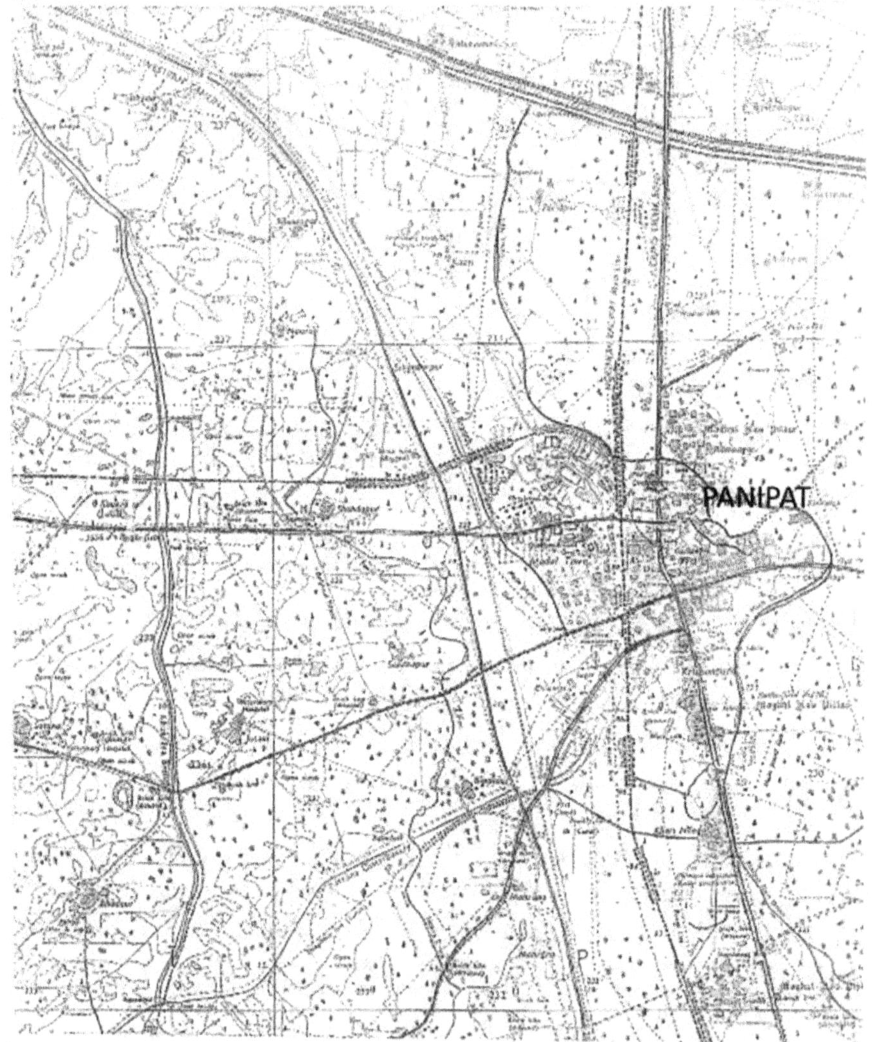

Fig. 3.1 Location Map of Panipat City [4]

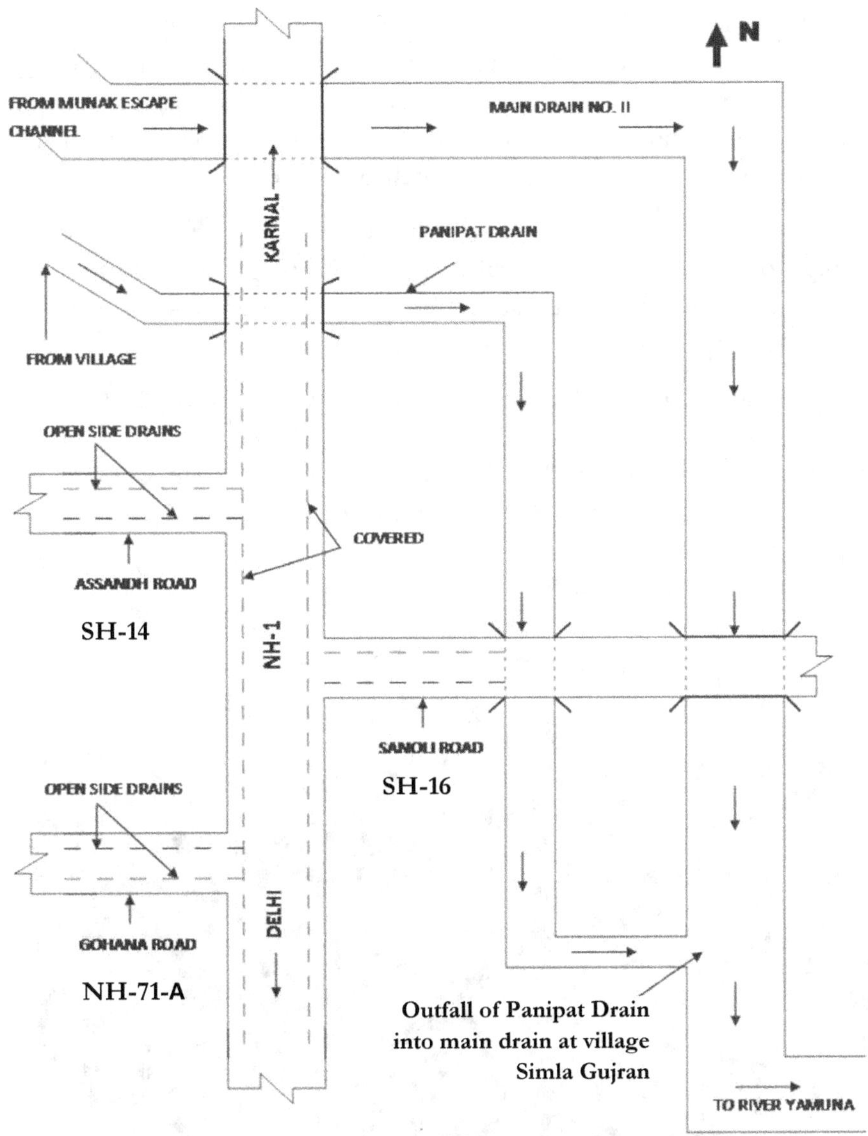

Fig. 3.2 Schematic diagram of roads and drainage system of Panipat
(not to scale)

From km 89.260 the water is taken south in the roadside drain and discharged into the existing storm water manhole at km 88.400, which is connected to the Panipat drain at a distance of 400 m towards the east. Between km 89.940 km 89.260, the water is discharged through the culvert

31

at km 89.586 into the existing storm water manhole at km 89.571. This manhole is connected through a pipe drain to the Panipat drain. From 88.380 the water is taken south and discharged through the culvert at km 86.985 into the Panipat drain. For the rest of the stretch, the storm water drains are connected to the nearest cross drainage works.

There is stagnation of water on the right side as well as left of the bridge of Panipat drain at RD.km.91.400 of NH-1 as shown in Plates 3.2 and 3.3. Mostly sullage water flows through the bridge. As a result it emanates foul smell and leads to growth of weeds and vegetations.

Besides this bridge, there are nine culverts crossing the NH-1. The water on both sides of most of these culverts remains stagnant as shown in case of one of the culverts in Plate 3.4. The problem of blocked water way is one of the reasons for deterioration of environment quality and breeding of mosquitoes, etc since there are various side drains and houses directly contacted to the Panipat drain.

Plate 3.1 Outfall of Panipat drain into main drain, Vill. Simla Gujran

Plate 3.2 Panipat drain crossing NH-1 at RD 91.400 km
(Panipat-Delhi Side)

Plate 3.3 Silting of Panipat drain at RD 91.400 km of NH-1
(Panipat Karnal Side)

Plate 3.4 Stagnant water near culvert (RD km 92.635) due to blocked waterway

3.3 WASTEWATER AND SURFACE RUN-OFF DISPOSAL

The wastewater generated in the city either accumulates or flows through Panipat drain which passes through the city. This drain acts as the carrier of polluted effluent of industries and city sewage. The surface run-off from roads is collected along the roadside through storm water drains and is discharged through cross drainage works in the Panipat drain.

3.4 EXISTING SEWERAGE SYSTEM

Presently only 35 to 40% of the city is covered by the sewerage system. The contributory area for wastewater collection for Panipat has been divided into two zones with G.T. Road (N.H.1) as the dividing line. Two-treatment plants of10 MLD and 35 MLD (millions liter per day) capacity have been constructed for Zone-I and Zone-II respectively under Yamuna Action Plan-1 during 1995-1998. Both treatment plants are based on UASB (up flow anaerobic sludge blanket) technology and are running satisfactorily. However, these are reportedly working under overloaded conditions. The treated effluent from the 10 MLD zone-1 treatment plant drain ultimately meets river Yamuna through drain no. 4 and drain no. 8. The treated effluent from 35 MLD Zone II treatment plant located at

Village Siwah is discharged into Panipat drain which ultimately meets River Yamuna through main drain no. 2. The river is again tapped at Wazirabad through a barrage for drinking water supply to Delhi.

The industrial activity of Panipat includes dyeing units, dairy units, and handloom units, etc which contribute to waste water in the municipal sewers. The sugar mill has its own wastewater treatment plant and HUDA proposes another common treatment plant for the textile industries under rehabilitation of dyeing unit plan at sector-29.

3.5 SOLID WASTE MANAGEMENT

Solid waste management is the responsibility of the municipal council. It is estimated that Panipat City generates about 100 mt of solid waste per day with the industries being the largest contributors. The council is experimenting with the handing over of 50% of its service areas to a private contractor for lifting and dumping. The city does not have a systematic disposal system with the collected garbage being dumped in the low lying areas of the city, usually near the railway lines and the vacant low lying plots as shown in Plate 3.5.

Plate 3.5 Solid waste dumped in low-lying plots near Mittal Mall

3.6 MAJOR ISSUES OF DRAINAGE IN PANIPAT

3.6.1 General Issues

(i)   Drainage system of Panipat city suffers from the problems of silting of drains, non-integration of various drains, blocked water way near culverts, blockages by various types of solid wastes and mixing of polluted effluents of industry and sewage into the storm water. Lack of regular cleaning and maintenance of drains also leads to poor drainage conditions in the city.

(ii)   Handloom industries that have traditionally formed the back bone of the economy have come up at random locations. This mixed land use has meant that there is no control over regulation of the wastes discharged into the drains leading to adverse environmental impacts.

(iii)   The smaller industrial units have no systematic means of disposing the wastes they generate with the result that wastes are discharged directly into the sewerage that carries domestic waste. This intermixing with sewage leads to blockages and presence of chemicals that in turn compromise the efficiency of the sewerage treatment plants.

(iv)   Solid waste disposal has been identified as a major problem. The representatives of various residents associations complain that wastes/garbage remain uncollected for months together in many areas in the town.

(v)   Panipat has a number of HUDA (Haryana Urban Development Authority) sectors that are located within the council limits. While the development of these sectors is complete, many of them have not been handed over to the council as yet. In fact there are no plans for a formal integration of these sectors with the council even for the sectors that have been handed over to the council. At present, the council does not seem to have the capacity in terms of manpower or infrastructure to handle the added responsibility.

3.6.2 Drainage Issues Related to Road Network of City

(i) About 50% of roads have side drains (Kuccha and Pucca) and remaining are without drains. Most of the drains are in a damaged condition.

(ii) The unorganized and scattered layout of these open drains leads to over flow during rainy season.

(iii) Due to absence of any sewerage system in many areas, these roadside open drains receive all sullage water, over flow from septic tanks and soakage pits and raw sewage along the NH-1 and other roads. This ultimately gets discharged into River Yamuna through Panipat drain and main drain causing contamination of water and health hazards.

(iv) It is observed during field observations that major portions of these Pucca drains require desilting and repairs. Most of the existing drains are covered with grass and mud. To function properly, desilting is an immediate requirement.

(v) New pucca drains need to be constructed, where they are not in existence along the road. Majority of the kuccha drains are of irregular section and need pucca lining to retain its hydraulic properties.

(vi) At many places drains are encroached by the buildings.

(vii) At many places, the inter connectivity between the drains does not exist.

(viii) It has been observed that maintenance of the drains is a neglected phenomenon. Solid waste is found in open drains thus choking the drains. Regular cleaning of the drains is not in practice.

(ix) Further, it is observed from the site reconnaissance that surface drains carrying polluted waste discharged into water bodies have choked the water bodies in localized areas. With strong presence of presence of foul smell, these water bodies give clear signs of high pollution level.

(x) The water from nearby industrial areas is discharged in to roadside drains illegally as shown in Plate 3.6.

(xi)   The construction waste is still lying in drains as depicted in Plate 3.7.

(xii)   There is only one stream known as Panipat drain into which the drainage is diverted and which is full of garbage, due to which the capacity of the drain has been reduced as shown in Plate 3.8.

(xiii)   Stagnation of water takes place during rains, Plate 3.9.

(xiv)   In rainy season, the garbage is found to have blocked the waterway at the location of a bridge, Plate 3.10.

(xv)   The road side drains on most of the roads are located beneath the approach passage of adjoining shops with intervening ground between roads and drains having adverse slope towards the road. This makes the drains redundant converting them as dumping places for garbage of the shops.

The roads like NH-1 have the side drains located by the edge of road pavement away from entry passage ramps of adjoining shops and are observed to have better road drainage.

Plate 3.6 Industrial water flowing in road side drain on N.H. 1

Plate 3.7 Solid waste existing in the drain

Plate 3.8 Different types of waste blocking the Panipat Drain near PWD office

Plate 3.9 Stagnation of water on NH -1 due to blockage of kerb inlets during rains

Plate 3.10: Blockage of Panipat drain during rainy season

4 DRAINAGE DATA OF PANIPAT ROADS

4.1 GENERAL

In order to fully understand existing conditions and develop the analytical tools, substantial amounts of data are to be collected. Data collected for the present study include (i) general data of the area including its climatic data and (ii) the road data. The road data have been collected for its geometrics, pavement type and its condition, size and bed slope of roadside drains, cross drainage works of the road and general drainage problems of the road. The data have been collected in respect of all the four main roads of the city considered in the present study as mentioned in section 1.4. The collected data are based on existing city records coupled with a field survey program that included measurement and determination of cross section elements of roads, slope of road side drains and their size, and details of cross drainage works. Levelling exercise was taken up in the field to determine the cross and longitudinal slope of the roads as well as bed slope of the drains. The data was collected in a manner so as to achieve the objectives of the study.

4.2 GENERAL DATA OF STUDY AREA

4.2.1 Soil Type

The area is marked by grayish sandy/silty soils all along the flat plain land. The soils are found to be well developed with good fertility. The soils in the area [5] generally consist of ML (silts of low plasticity), CL-ML (clays of low plasticity to silt of low plasticity) or SM (silty sands) type. The CBR (California bearing ratio) value of the soils [5] under 4-days soaked condition varies from about 3.0 to 4.5 %.

4.2.2 Meteorological Data

The study area falls under semi-arid climatic zone of India marked by three distinct seasons, namely summer, winter and rainy season. Summer is characterized by high temperature reaching up to 43-45°C during May and June months. During winter season the temperature reduces drastically and is lowest during January and February months with mean minimum temperature about 2 to 3°C.

4.2.3 Rainfall Data

The most critical component of climate for roads is rainfall. The rainfall in Haryana is highly variable and erratic. The study area lies in the semi arid zone based on the Koppen climate classification flow chart [6]. The major portion of the rainfall comes from the Southwest monsoon. The mean annual rainfall is between 400 to 650mm

The rainfall data for the last 12 years was collected from the office of Deputy Commissioner, Panipat and is given in table 4.1. The map of India [7] exhibited in fig. 4.1 showing state-wise average rainfall distribution depicts that Haryana falls in the range of 1-500 mm rainfall.

4.2.4 Topography

Topography controls the flow regime of a river. Landscape of the study area is totally flat with elevation varying from 233 to 230 m above AMSL (average mean sea level) over 7 km distance from North to South. The streams/nallah flow from North to South in general, but locally, the drainage in the Northern part is towards East and in the Southern parts it is west to south-west, the swing being at the toll (octroi) on Sanoli road, just North of Chadanibagh area.

Table 4.1 Month and Year wise rainfall (in mm) in Panipat

S. No.	Year	Jan	Feb	Mar	Apr	May	Jun	July	Aug	Sep	Oct	Nov	Dec	Total
1	1997	9	-	12.5	64.5	28	77.5	167	216.5	29	87.5	24	57	772.5
2	1998	-	26	30	3.5	10.5	23	150	155	97.5	98	8	-	601.5
3	1999	37.5	-	-	-	79	80	104	40	99	-	-	-	439.5
4	2000	22	59	-	-	7	79	140	77	18	-	-	-	402
5	2001	24	5	12	18	-	146	105	100	16	2	-	-	428
6	2002	44	10	6	-	27.5	26	7.5	50	119	-	-	1	291
7	2003	16	22	-	-	18	24	87	81	98	-	-	6	352
8	2004	49	-	-	10	26	34	25	325	71	31	-	-	571
9	2005	16	22	53	-	5	15	38	71	296	-	-	-	516
10	2006	3	-	30	-	2	90	243	20	19	-	-	-	407
11	2007	-	56	27	1	8	75	49.5	46	85	-	-	-	347.5
12	2008	-	2	-	2	45	104	193	132	141	-	-	-	619
Average		18.4	17	14.2	8.2	21.3	64.5	109	109.5	90.7	18.2	2.7	5.3	479

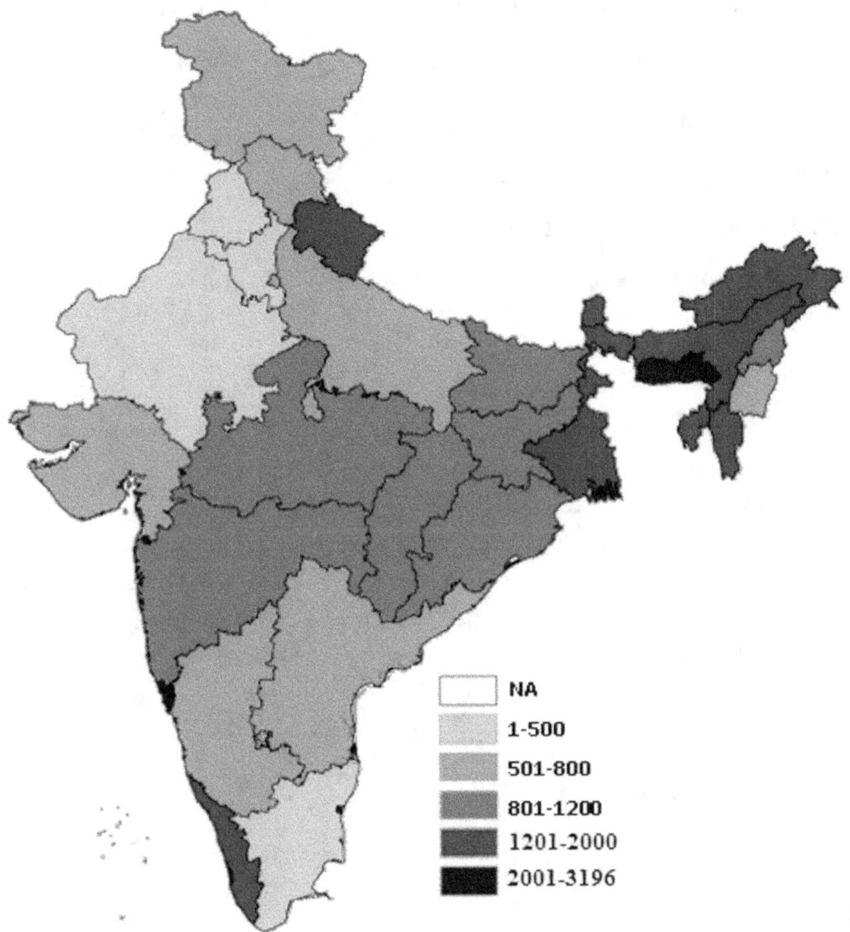

Fig. 4.1 State wise Average Rainfall Distribution in India (in mm)

4.2.5 Humidity

Relative humidity in the region varies from 70 % to 80 %.

4.2.6 Land Use

The vast stretch of the area is highly urbanized and industrialized, while the hinterland comprises agricultural land. Wheat, sugarcane and paddy are the main crops. A major irrigation canal "Western Yamuna" runs west of the city from North to South. Horticulture is limited to pomegranate, guava, etc.

4.3   ROAD DATA FOR VARIOUS ROADS UNDER STUDY

Road data for its geometrics, pavement type and its condition, drain size and its bed slope, cross drainage works and general drainage problems of the road in respect of four selected main roads of the city were observed by field studies. The data for the roads under study are given as under.

4.3.1   Road Data for NH-1 (G.T. Road)

Plates 4.1 and 4.2 exhibit the view of NH-1. The road data are given as under:

(i) <u>Road Reference data</u>

Name of Road	: Sher Shah Suri Marg or Grand Trunk road
Category of road	: National Highway (NH-1)
Length of stretch studied	: 10 km (RD 86 to 96 km)

Details of the road stretch : The studied stretch is a part of NH-1 between km 86-96 encompassing Panipat city. The road stretch falls predominantly in urban section of the city. The central portion of city with intense developmental activities is between km 89 to 93. The balance portion of the stretch has scattered development with residential, commercial and industrial belt on either side of the road.

(ii) <u>Road geometric details</u>

Road land width	: 68 m
Road way width	: 48.5 m
Carriage way width	: 40 m

No of lanes   : Main carriageway is six-lanes divided and peripheral carriageway is two lanes on either side of main carriageway.

Terrain type   : The area is monotonously flat with slopes less than 2% in general

Camber / cross slope (Plate 4.3 and 4.4)

	: Carriageway = 2.5 %
	: Footpath, divider = 3.5 %
Gradient	: Almost flat
Cross section	: It is shown in fig. 4.2.

Plate 4.1   A View of elevated stretch of NH-1

Plate 4.2   A View of leveled stretch of NH-1

(iii) <u>Road geometric details</u>

Road land width	: 68 m
Road way width	: 48.5 m
Carriage way width	: 40 m
No of lanes	: Main carriageway is six-lanes divided and peripheral carriageway is two lanes on either side of main carriageway.
Terrain type	: The area is monotonously flat with slopes less than 2% in general
Camber / cross slope	: Carriageway = 2.5 %
	Footpath, divider = 3.5 %
(plate 4.3 and 4.4)	
Gradient	: Almost flat
Cross section	: It is shown in fig. 4.2.

(iv) <u>Road pavement condition and surface type</u>

Extent of cracking	: Very less
Extent of potholes	: Not seen
Surface type	: Bituminous
Shoulder type	: Paved / Bituminous

(v) <u>Pavement composition</u>

Bituminous concrete	: 50 mm
Dense bituminous macadam	: 165 mm
Wet mix macadam	: 250 mm
Granular sub base	: 230 mm
Total thickness	: 695 mm

(vi) Data of existing drains

Type of drain   : Rectangular, cement concrete

Size of drain   : 1 m x 1 m

Average slope of drain   : 1 in 675
bed

Location on road   : Under footpath, totally covered

Manholes   : At regular intervals

Inlets   : Kerb inlets are provided at intervals of 30 m. A
                                              PVC pipe of 20 cm dia is provided at the kerb
                                              line to connect the drain.

(vii) Cross drainage structures

Drainage is mainly through the Panipat drain, which crosses NH-1 at km 91.400. Besides this bridge, there are 11 culverts / pipe culverts in the studied stretch. A brief description of the culverts is given in table 4.2.

During the field survey and data collection process, the existing cross drainage structures and adequacy of water way provided under the bridges have been studied. The data on flood discharges adopted for the design of these culverts were not available with the concerned departments.

There were no noticeable HFL marks in any stream / culvert / bridge section. Even the catchment areas are not well defined, as stream flow is restricted to urban habitation. The cross drainage structures are shown in Plates 4.3 to 4.12.

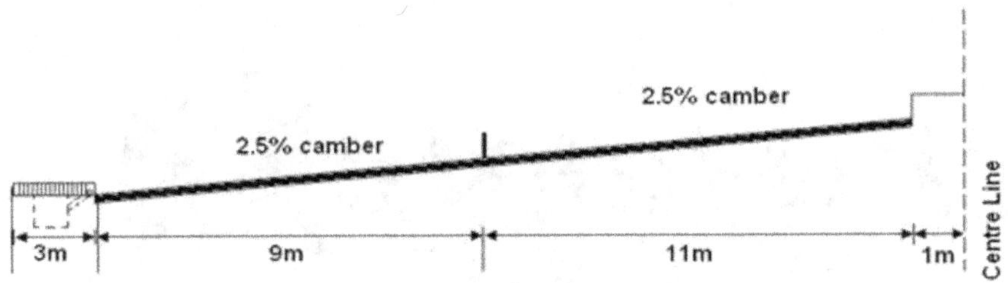

Fig. 4.2 Cross section of NH-1

Table 4.2 Existing Culverts in Studied Stretch of NH-1

S. No.	RD (km)	Type of culvert	Location on NH-1
1	86.120	Box culvert of 1 cell of 2 m	Opp. Janta Hospital Nangal Kheri
2	86.271	Box culvert of 2 cells of 2 m each	Nangal Kheri Village-Road
3	86.490	Box culvert of 2 cells of 3 m each	Truck Parking Lay Bye
4	86.603	Box culvert of 2 cells of 2 m each	Opp. Bajaj Paints N.F.L. Road
5	86.945	Slab culvert of 3 spans 2 m each	Before ITI College
6	88.397	2 pipes of 0.8 m dia	Opp. Surya Highway Inn.
7	89.915	1 pipe of 1.2 m dia	SBI Bank left Sunil handloom right
8	91.400	New Bridge on the peripheral road of 3 spans of 8.9 m each	Near PWD rest house
9	92.635	Culvert of 2 spans of 3 m each	Opp.Parnami Plaza
10	93.022	Box culvert of 1 cell of 2 m each	Dinesh Mills
11	95.130	Box culvert of 1 cell of 2.5 m	Near Traffic aid centre

Plate 4.3 Camber observations on NH-1

Plate 4.4 Box culvert of one cell of 2m at km 86.120 of NH-1

Plate 4.5 Box culvert of two cells of 2m at km 86.271 of NH-1

Plate 4.6 Box culvert of 2-cells of 3 m width at Km 86.490 of NH-1

Plate 4.7 Box culvert of 2 cells of 2m at km 86.603 of NH-1

Plate 4.8 Box culvert of 3 spans of 2m at km 86.945 of NH-1

Plate 4.9 Two pipes of 0.8 m dia at km 88.397 of NH-1

Plate 4.10 Bridge, 3-spans of 8.9 m each, at km 91.400, L-side

Plate 4.11 Culvert of two spans of 3m each at km. 92.635

Plate 4.12 Box culvert of one cell of 2m at Km. 93.022

(viii) <u>General Drainage Problems of NH-1</u>

There are various drainage problems noticed during field study:

(a) Rain causes drains to overflow and renders road under knee deep water, which creates problem for road users. The drainage system gets clogged and the road at different places becomes waterlogged for several hours.

(b) There is only one stream known as Panipat drain into which the storm water drainage is diverted. This drain is partly full of garbage due to which capacity of the drain has got reduced. The garbage in the drains includes leaves, plastic bags, cans, plastic bottle / curtains, construction material, etc which block the drains.

(c) At some locations where storm water drains meet the intercepting drain, effluent from industrial units and residential colonies also enters the storm water drainage.

(d) At some locations, the water on both sides of the cross drainage work remains stagnant as there is no connectivity to Panipat drain as shown in plate 4.11 which results into a breeding point for mosquitoes and deterioration of environmental quality.

(e) It is observed during field study that major portions of these drains require desilting and minor repairs.

(f) Due to coverage of drains, maintenance of these drains is neglected. Regular maintenance is not in practice.

(g) The kerb inlets at some locations were found choked.

(h) The waste construction material is still lying in the drains.

(i) Fallen trees, construction material, vegetation and slush, etc block the waterways of cross drainage works.

4.3.2 Road Data for Panipat Gohana Road (NH-71 A)

(i) <u>Road Reference data</u>

Name of Road	: Gohana Road
Category of road	: National Highway (NH-71A)
Length of stretch studied	: 3 km (RD Km 0-3)
Details of the road stretch	: As the road passes through the city there are many types of habitations located on either side of the road such as residential colonies, hospitals, shops, service stations and industrial units. A railway over bridge is also situated on the road.

(ii) <u>Road geometric details</u>

Road land width	: 36.5 m
Road way width	: 12 m
Carriage way width	: 9 m
No of lanes	: Main carriageway is 2-lane undivided
Terrain type	: The area is almost flat with slopes less than 2% in general
Camber / cross slope	: Carriageway = 1.5 %
Gradient	: Almost flat
Cross section	: It is shown in fig. 4.3

(iii) <u>Road pavement condition and surface type</u>

Extent of cracking	: Very high (Plate 4.13)
Extent of potholes	: Very high
Surface type	: Bituminous
Shoulder type	: Earthen with higher level than road at many

places

(iv) Pavement composition

Premix carpet, PC	: 20 mm
Bituminous macadam	: 110 mm
Water Bound Macadam	: 250 mm
Granular sub base	: Nil
Total thickness	: 380 mm

(v) Data of existing drains

Type of drain	: Rectangular, cement concrete, open type
Size of drain	: 0.60 m x 0.40 m
Average slope of drain bed	: 1 in 675
Location on road	: Both sides of the road
Manholes	: At regular intervals
Inlets	: Not existing
Drain condition	There is no connectivity between various lengths of the drains. The drains have been closed due to construction activities and access ramps made by the houses and industrial units situated on the road.

(vi) Cross drainage structures

The flow of roadside drains on both side of the road up to ROB is from west to east. The drains discharge the water into the drain of NH-1. Beyond the ROB there is no connectivity and the water remains accumulated in low-lying areas such as parks, private plots, etc. There are no cross drainage works in the studied stretch of the road.

(vii) General Drainage Problems of NH-71A

(a) At many locations, the shoulders are higher than the edge of the road. The water remains stagnant on the road for several hours.

(b) The slope provided in the drain is inadequate. The water remains standstill in the drains.

(c) The desilting of the drains is very cumbersome as these are covered by slabs cast by shopkeepers, industrialists as per their convenience.

(d) The drains on this road are discontinuous.

(e) Road shoulders are encroached by shopkeepers, industrialists for their commercial activities.

(f) Dumping of garbage at the roadside is a common phenomenon, which spills into the drains to clog them.

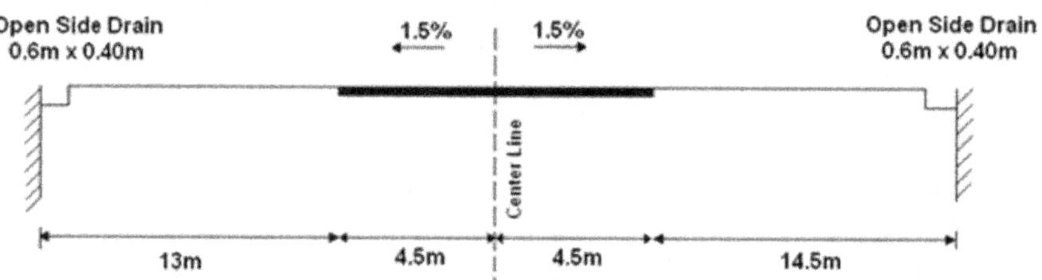

Fig. 4.3 Cross section of Panipat-Gohana Road, NH-71-A

Plate 4.13 A view of NH-71-A, Panipat-Gohana Road

4.3.3 Road Data for Panipat Assandh Road, SH-14

(i)   <u>Road Reference data</u>

Name of Road	: Assandh Road
Category of road	: State Highway (SH-14)
Length of stretch studied	: 2.4 km (RD km 0-2.4)
Details of the road stretch	: This is an important road connecting Panipat to Jind. It takes off at 90.600 km towards west of NH 1. There is also an ROB between km 0.180 to km 0.940 of Assandh road. Shops, hospitals, petrol pumps, residential houses are situated on both sides of the road.

(ii)   <u>Road geometric details</u>

Road land width	: 18.5 m
Road way width	: 12 m
Carriage way width	: 9 m
No of lanes	: Main carriageway is 2-lane undivided
Terrain type	: The area is almost flat with slopes less than 2% in general
Camber / cross slope	: Carriageway = 2%, shoulder = 3.0 %
Gradient	: Almost flat
Cross section	: It is shown in fig. 4.4

(iii)   <u>Road pavement condition and surface type</u>

Extent of cracking	: Moderate (Plate 4.14)
Extent of potholes	: Moderate
Surface type	: Bituminous
Shoulder type	: Paved / bituminous

(iv)   <u>Pavement composition</u>

Premix carpet, PC	: 20 mm
Bituminous macadam	: 155 mm
Water Bound Macadam	: 150 mm
Granular sub base	: Nil
Total thickness	: 325 mm

(v) Data of existing drains

Type of drain	: Rectangular, brick masonry, open type
Size of drain	: 0.60 m x 0.30 m
Average slope of drain bed	: 1 in 750
Location on road	: Both sides of the road
Manholes	: At regular intervals
Inlets	: Do not exist
Drain condition	There is no connectivity between various lengths of the drains. The drains have been closed due to construction activities and access ramps made by the houses and shops situated on the road.

(vi) Cross drainage structures

The water from the road side drain from ROB to NH-1 is discharged into the side drain of NH-1 and beyond ROB the water discharges into low lying areas along the railway line which further connects to the Panipat drain. There are no cross drainage works in the studied stretch of the road.

(vii) General Drainage Problems of SH-14

(a) The drains are filled up with garbage resulting into reduction of capacity.

(b) Slope in drain is inadequate as a result of which the water remains standstill in the drains.

(c) Sewerage and household waste is discharged at some locations into the roadside drains.

(d) There is lack of connectivity in various portions of drains.

(e) The drains are not properly maintained and lack regular cleaning.

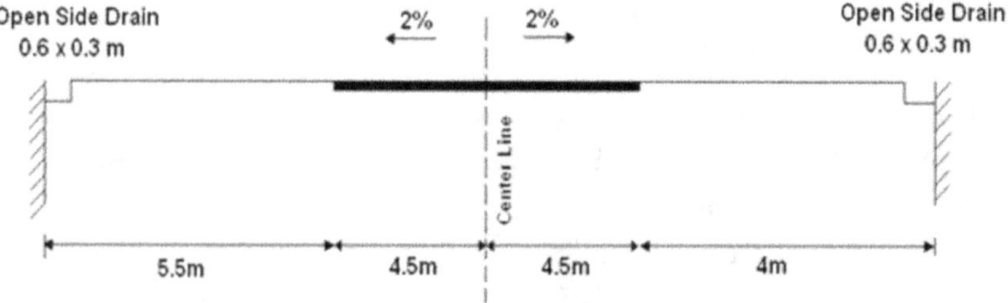

Fig. 4.4 Cross section of Panipat-Assandh Road, SH-14

Plate 4.14 A view of SH-14, Panipat-Assandh Road

4.3.4 Road Data for Panipat Shamli Meerut Road, SH-16 (Sanoli Road)

(i) <u>Road Reference data</u>

Name of Road	: Sanoli Road
Category of road	: State Highway (SH-16)
Length of stretch studied	: 3.0 km (RD km 0-3)
Details of the road stretch	: This road connects Panipat to important cities of Uttar Pradesh such as Shamli, Mujjafarnagar, Haridwar etc. There are various dying units, hospitals, hotels, service stations, banks, residential colonies etc. on both sides of the road.

(ii) <u>Road geometric details</u>

Road land width	: 23.9 m
Road way width	: 19 m
Carriageway width	: 14 m
No of lanes	: Main carriageway is 4-lane divided (Fig. 4.5)
Terrain type	: The area is almost flat with slopes less than

                    2% in general

Camber / cross slope   : Carriageway = 2%, shoulder = 3.0 %

Gradient   : Almost flat

Cross section   : It is shown in fig. 4.5

(iii) <u>Road pavement condition and surface type</u>

Extent of cracking   : High (plate 4.15)

Extent of potholes   : High

Surface type   : Bituminous / Cement concrete

Shoulder type   : Brick paved

(iv) <u>Pavement composition</u>

Premix carpet, PC   : 20 mm

Bituminous macadam   : 155 mm

Water Bound Macadam   : 150 mm

Granular sub base   : Nil

Total thickness   : 305 mm

(v) <u>Data of existing drains</u>

Type of drain   : Rectangular, brick masonry, open type

Size of drain   : 0.75 m x 0.60 m

Average slope of drain bed   : 1 in 925

Location on road   : Both sides of the road

Manholes   : At regular intervals

Inlets   : Do not exist

Drain condition   There is no connectivity between various lengths of the drains. The drains have been closed due to construction activities and access ramps made by the houses and shops situated on the road.

(vi) <u>Cross drainage structures</u>

There is only Panipat drain, which crosses the road at RD 2.4 of Sanoli Road (plate 4.16). The roadside drains discharge water into the Panipat drain near Chandni Bagh area.

(vii) <u>General drainage problem of SH-16</u>

(a) At many places drain are encroached by the buildings.

(b) The drains are open and filled with mud, plastic bags, plastic bottles and other domestic wastes.

(c) At some locations, the drains are blocked by some construction activities.

(d) The edges of drains are broken at some locations.

(e) Sewerage disposal from nearby residential areas are connected with these road side drain due to which the drain are filled up with slush and capacity of the drains have been reduced up to 50%.

(f) The water remains stand still that causes various diseases to the people living nearby.

(g) Solid waste has been thrown into the drains.

(h) Maintenance is a neglected phenomenon.

(i) The drains are incapable to hold water during rainy season for several hours.

(j) The ugly sight of dumped garbage at road corners of Sanoli road is causing problems for the commuters and residents of the area. It has become a virtual health hazard and source of environmental pollution. The garbage remains spilled over on the road and then enters into open drains that make them clogged.

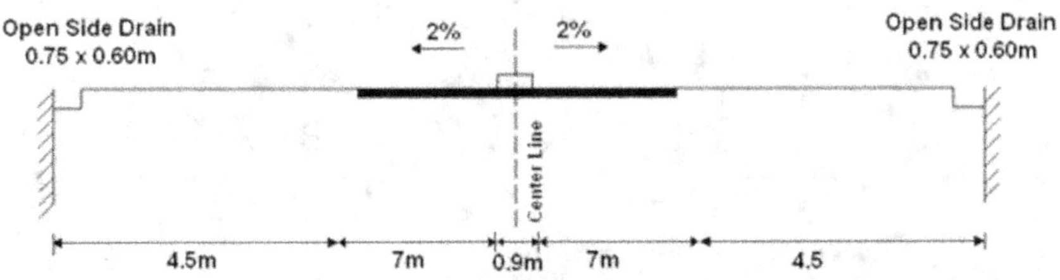

Fig. 4.5 Cross section of Panipat-Shamli Road, SH-16

Plate 4.15 A view of SH-16, Panipat-Shamli Road

Plate 4.16 Panipat Drain Crossing SH-16 at Km 2.4

5   DESIGN OF ROAD SIDE DRAINAGE SYSTEM

5.1   GENERAL

Design of roadside drains has been taken up in this chapter for all the four main roads of the city selected for this study. The design of drains has been carried out using rational method of design as discussed earlier in chapter-II. Design discharge has been determined for critical intensity of rainfall of duration equal to time of concentration. Rectangular drains are designed keeping in view that the same type of drains are actually provided on the roadside. The designed sections of the drains are compared with actual sections of drains provided on the roads to judge the adequacy of the roadside drainage. An attempt has also been made to evolve a simplified procedure for the purpose of design of roadside drains.

5.2   DESIGN OF ROAD SIDE DRAIN OF NH-1 (KM 86.945 TO 86.600)

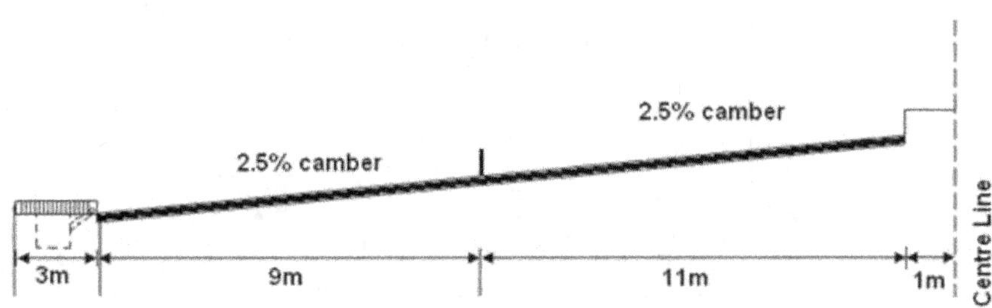

Fig. 5.1 Cross section of NH-1 at km 86.800

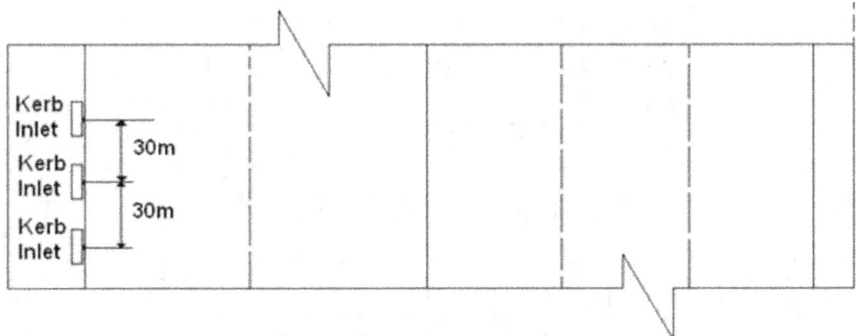

Fig. 5.2 Plan of NH-1 at km 86.800

5.2.1 Given Data of Road and Road Side Drain

Slope of bituminous surface	= 0.025 (equal to camber)
Width of paved surface (fig. 5.1)	= 24 m
Spacing of kerb inlets (fig. 5.2)	= 30 m
Gradient in the kerb channel	= 1 in 300
Size of road side drain provided	= 1.0 m x 1.0 m (rectangular)
Slope of drain bed	= 1 in 675
Length of road side drain	= 345 m (up to cross drainage)

5.2.2 Calculation of Time of Concentration and Critical Rainfall Intensity

Time of concentration $t_c = t_1 + t_2 + t_3$

Where

t_1 = time of flow of water on the road surface in transverse direction in hrs

t_2 = time of flow of water in the kerb channel in longitudinal direction up to the point of inlet in hrs

t_3 = time of flow of water in the drain in longitudinal direction up to the point of outlet into a cross drain in hrs

Time of concentration has been calculated using equation (2.1). The calculations are given in table 5.1. Time of concentration from the table is found to be 23.8 minutes.

Table 5.1 Time of Concentration for NH-1

Section	Direction of Flow	L (km)	H (m)	t_1 (hrs)	t_2 (hrs)	t_3 (hrs)	t_c (hrs)	Speed (m/s)
Road surface	Transverse	0.021	0.525	0.014	-	-	-	0.42
Kerb channel	Longitudinal	0.030	0.1	-	0.040	-	-	0.21
Drain	Longitudinal	0.345	0.51			0.359	-	0.27
Time of concentration t_c (hrs) = $t_1 + t_2 + t_3$ =							0.413hr=24.8 mts	

Average speed of water on road = 51 / (0.054 x 3600) = 0.26 m/sec

Speed of water in drain = 345/(0.359x 3600) = 0.27 m/sec

Alternatively, time of concentration can be calculated by speed of water also

t_c (minutes) = (51/0.27) x 1/60 + L/(0.27x60)

= 3.15 + (L /16.2)

L (flow distance in drain, metres) = (t_c −3.15) x 16.2

A (Area contributing to flow upto L m in hect)

= (24 x L)/10000

= [24 (t_c −3.15) x 16.2] / 10000

The values of L for different values of time of concentration and area are calculated using above relationships. These are given in table 5.2.

Table 5.2 Values of flow distance in drain 'L' and catchment area 'A' for different values of Time of concentration

t_c (mts)	10	15	20	30	40	50	60	90	120
L (m)	111	192	273	435	597	759	921	1407	1893
A (hect)	0.27	0.46	0.66	1.04	1.43	1.82	2.21	3.38	4.54

For the given case of NH-1, the value of L is 345 m, which gives a concentration time of about 24 minutes. However, a concentration time of 30 minutes seems to be more appropriate considering the variation in the inlet spacing and the location of the cross drain / culvert on the road. Further design, therefore, is checked based upon the concentration time of 30 minutes.

From rainfall maps of India [8], one-hour maximum rainfall near Delhi is given in table 5.3.

Table 5.3 One hour maximum rainfall near Delhi [8]

Frequency (T)	Rainfall in for one hour (cm)	Conversion factor (F) (w.r.t. 2 year frequency)
2 years	3.6 cm	1
5 years	5.5 cm	1.53
10 years	6.2 cm	1.72
25 years	8.0 cm	2.22
50 years	9.2 cm	2.56

Now conversion factors [6] for converting one-hr rainfall intensity to intensity of other durations for 2 yr frequency storm are given in table 5.4.

Table 5.4 Conversion factors for rainfall intensity other than one hr [8]

Duration of rainfall (mins)	5	10	15	20	30	40	50	60	90	120
Rainfall intensity (cm/hr)	13.32	10.26	8.64	7.49	6.01	4.79	4.21	3.6	3.0	2.4
Conversion factor	3.7	2.85	2.4	2.08	1.67	1.33	1.17	1.0	0.83	0.67

5.2.3   Determination of Design Discharge

Discharge as given by eq. (2.3), Q	= 0.028 PAIc cum/sec
Coefficient of Runoff, P	= 0.9 (table 2.3)
Area of catchment, A	= 24x345/10000 = 0.828 hect

For t_c = 30 min, critical intensity of rainfall from table 5.4, Ic
$$= 6.01 \text{ cm/hr}$$

Therefore, Q (for 2 yr frequency)	= .028x0.9x0.828x6.01=0.125cum/sec
Q for 25 yr frequency (table 5.3)	= 0.125 x 2.22 = 0.278 cum/sec

Adding 25% for discharge from intermediate drains, design discharge Q

for 02 yr frequency	= 0.125 x 1.25 = 0.156 cum/sec
for 25 yr frequency	= 0.278 x 1.25 = 0.348 cum/sec

5.2.4   Drain Section Calculations

Assume a rectangular drain x-section of 60 cm (width) x 50 cm (depth)

Free board	= 15 cm (from table 2.6)
Depth of flow	= 50-15 = 35 cm
Area of cross section of flow, A	= 0.6 x 0.35 = 0.21 m²
Wetted perimeter, p	= 0.6+0.35+0.35 = 1.3 m
Hydraulic mean radius, R= A/p	= 0.162 m

Gradient of drain bed, S $\quad$ = 1 in 675

Manning's 'n' value (for plastered brick surface, table 2.4)

$\quad$ = 0.015

As per eq. (2.4), mean velocity, V $\quad = V = (1/n) R^{2/3} S^{1/2}$

$\quad$ = 0.761 m/sec

$\quad$ (OK as per table 2.5)

Discharge, Q from eq. (2.5) $\quad$ = A x V = 0.21x0.761 = 0.16 cum/sec, which is more than 0.156 cum/sec. This size is therefore OK for 02 yr frequency storm.

Assume another trial x-section of 100 cm (width) x 55 cm (depth)

Free board $\quad$ = 15 cm (from table 2.6)

Depth of flow $\quad$ = 55-15 = 40 cm

Area of cross section of flow, A $\quad$ = 1.0 x 0.4 = 0.4 m2

Wetted perimeter, p $\quad$ = 1.0+0.4+0.4 = 1.8 m

Hydraulic mean radius, R=A/p $\quad$ = 0.222 m

Gradient of drain bed, S $\quad$ = 1 in 675

Manning's 'n' value (for plastered brick surface, table 2.4)

$\quad$ = 0.015

As per eq. (2.4), mean velocity, V $\quad = V = (1/n) R^{2/3} S^{1/2}$

$\quad$ = 0.941 m/sec

$\quad$ (OK as per table 2.5)

Discharge, Q from eq. (2.5) $\quad$ = A x V = 0.4x0.941 = 0.377 cum/sec, which is more than 0.348 cum/sec. Therefore, drain size of 1.0 m x 0.55 m would be adequate for 25 yr frequency discharge.

Actual drain size already provided $\quad$ = 1.0 m x 1.0 m, which is OK for 25 yr frequency discharge.

5.3 DESIGN OF ROAD SIDE DRAIN FOR NH-71A (GOHANA ROAD

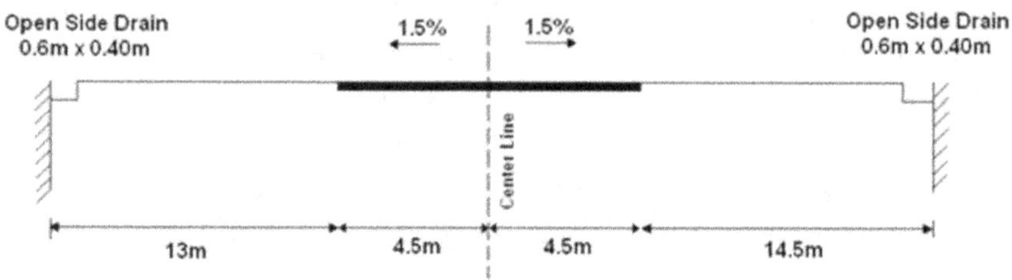

Fig. 5.3 Cross section of NH-71-A near Sugar Mill

5.3.1 Given Data of Road and Road Side Drain

Slope of bituminous surface	= 0.015 (equal to camber)
Width of paved surface (fig. 5.3)	= 4.5 m
Width of shoulder (fig. 5.3)	= 14.5 m (includes adjoining land
Spacing of kerb inlets	= No kerbs
Gradient in the kerb channel	= NA
Size of road side drain provided	= 0.6 m x 0.4 m (rectangular)
Slope of drain bed	= 1 in 675
Length of road side drain	= 500 m (up to cross drainage)

5.3.2 Calculation of Time of Concentration and Critical Rainfall Intensity

Time of concentration has been calculated in a similar manner as discussed in section 5.2. It is given in table 5.5.

Table 5.5 Time of Concentration for NH-71A

Section	Direction of Flow	L (km)	H (m)	t_1 (hrs)	t_2 (hrs)	t_3 (hrs)	t_c (hrs)	Speed (m/s)
Road surface	Transverse	0.019	0.285	0.016	-	-	-	0.33
Kerb channel	Longitudinal	-	-	-	-	-	-	-
-Drain	Longitudinal	0.5	0.741			0.478	-	0.29
	Time of concentration t_c (hrs) = $t_1 + t_2 + t_3$ =						0.493hr=29.6 mts	

Average speed of water on road	$=19 / (0.016 \times 3600) = 0.33$ m/sec
Speed of water in drain	$= 500/(0.478 \times 3600) = 0.29$ m/sec

Alternatively, time of concentration can be calculated by speed of water also

t_c (minutes)	$= (19/0.33) \times 1/60 + L / (0.29 \times 60)$
	$= 0.96 + (L /17.4)$
L (flow distance in drain, metres)	$= (t_c - 0.96) \times 17.4$
A (Area contributing to flow upto L m in hect)	
	$= (19 \times L)/10000$
	$= [19 (t_c - 0.96) \times 17.4] / 10000$

The values of L and area A for different values of time of concentration are calculated using above relationships. These are given in table 5.6.

Table 5.6 Values of flow distance in drain 'L' and catchment area 'A' for different values of Time of concentration

t_c (mts)	10	15	20	30	40	50	60	90	120
L (m)	157	244	331	505	679	853	1027	1549	2071
A (hect)	0.30	0.46	0.63	0.96	1.29	1.62	1.95	2.94	3.94

For the given case of NH-71A the value of L is 500 m, which gives a concentration time of about 30 minutes. Further design, therefore, is checked based upon the concentration time of 30 minutes.

5.3.3 Determination of Design Discharge

Discharge as given by eq. (2.3), Q	$= 0.028 \, PAIc$ cum/sec
Coefficient of Runoff, P (table 2.3, Fig. 5.3)	$= (0.9 \times 4.5 + 0.3 \times 14.5)/(4.5 + 14.5) = 0.44$
Area of catchment, A	$= 19 \times 500/10000 = 0.95$ hect
For $t_c = 30$ min, critical intensity of rainfall from table 4.4, Ic	$= 6.01$ cm/hr
Therefore, Q (for 2 yr frequency)	$= 0.028 \times 0.44 \times 0.95 \times 6.01$ $= 0.07$ cum/sec

Q for 25 yr frequency (table 5.3)   = 0.07 x 2.22 = 0.156 cum/sec

Adding 25% for discharge from intermediate drains, design discharge Q

	for 02 yr frequency	= 0.07 x 1.25 = 0.088 cum/sec
	for 25 yr frequency	= 0.156 x 1.25 = 0.195 cum/sec

5.3.4 Drain Section Calculations

Assume a rectangular drain x-section of 60 cm (width) x 40 cm (depth)

Free board	= 15 cm (from table 2.6)
Depth of flow	= 40-15 = 25 cm
Area of cross section of flow, A	= 0.6 x 0.25 = 0.15m²
Wetted perimeter, p	= 0.6+0.25+0.25 = 1.1 m
Hydraulic mean radius, R=A/p	= 0.136 m
Gradient of drain bed, S	= 1 in 675

Manning's 'n' value (for plastered brick surface, table 2.4)
= 0.015

As per eq. (2.4), mean velocity, V
$= V = (1/n) R^{2/3} S^{1/2} = 0.679$ m/sec
(OK as per table 2.5)

Discharge, Q from eq. (2.5)
$= A \times V = 0.15 \times 0.679$
= 0.102 cum/sec, which is more than 0.088 but less than 0.195 cum/sec

Actual drain size provided
= 0.6 m x 0.4 m.
This size is OK for 2 yr storm frequency but inadequate for 25 yr frequency.

Assume another trial section of 60 cm (width) x 60 cm (depth)

Free board	= 15 cm (from table 2.6)
Depth of flow	= 60-15 = 45 cm
Area of cross section of flow, A	= 0.6 x 0.45 = 0.27m²

Wetted perimeter, p	$= 0.6+0.45+0.45 = 1.5$ m
Hydraulic mean radius, R=A/p	$= 0.18$ m
Gradient of drain bed, S	$= 1$ in 675
Manning's 'n' value (for plastered brick surface, table 2.4)	$= 0.015$
As per eq. (2.4), mean velocity, V	$= V=(1/n) \, R^{2/3} S^{1/2}=0.818$ m/sec (OK as per table 2.5)
Discharge, Q from eq. (2.5)	$= A \times V = 0.27 \times 0.818$ $= 0.221$ cum/sec, which is more than 0.195 cum/sec

Therefore, for storm frequency of 25 years, a section of 0.6 m x 0.6 m would be adequate.

5.4 DESIGN OF SIDE DRAIN FOR PANIPAT ASSANDH ROAD, SH-14

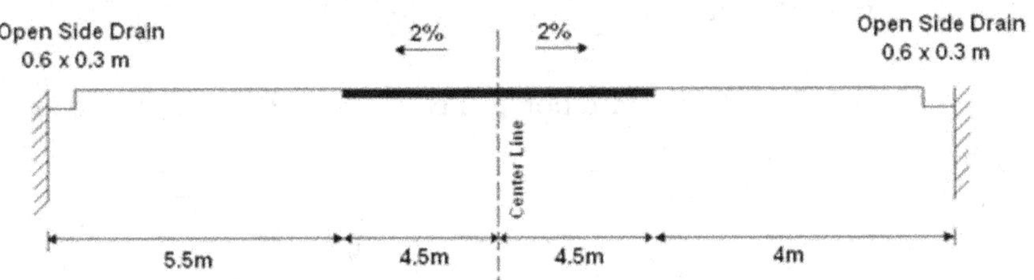

Fig. 5.4 Cross section of SH-14, Panipat Assandh Road

5.4.1 Given Data of Road and Road Side Drain

Slope of bituminous surface	$= 0.02$ (equal to camber)
Width of paved surface (fig. 5.4)	$= 4.5$ m
Width of shoulder (fig. 5.4)	$= 5.5$ m (includes adjoining land)
Spacing of kerb inlets	$= $ No kerbs
Gradient in the kerb channel	$= $ NA
Size of road side drain provided	$= 0.6$ m x 0.3 m (rectangular)
Slope of drain bed	$= 1$ in 750
Length of road side drain up to cross drainage	$= 500$ m

5.4.2 Calculation of Time of Concentration and Critical Rainfall Intensity

Time of concentration has been calculated in a similar manner as discussed in section 5.2. It is given in table 5.7.

Table 5.7 Time of Concentration for SH-14

Section	Direction of Flow	L (km)	H (m)	t_1 (hrs)	t_2 (hrs)	t_3 (hrs)	t_c (hrs)	Speed (m/s)
Road surface	Transverse	0.01	0.2	0.009	-	-	-	0.31
Kerb channel	Longitudinal	-	-	-	-	-	-	-
-Drain	Longitudinal	0.5	0.67			0.497	-	0.28
Time of concentration t_c (hrs) = t_1 + t_2 + t_3 =							0.506hr=30.4 mts	

Average speed of water on road =10 / (0.009 x 3600)=0.31 m/sec

Speed of water in drain = 500/(0.497x 3600) = 0.28 m/sec

Alternatively, time of concentration can be calculated by speed of water also

t_c (minutes) = (10/0.31) x 1/60 + L / (0.28x60)

= 0.54 + (L /16.8)

L (flow distance in drain, metres) = (t_c -0.54) x 16.8

A (Area contributing to flow upto L m in hect) = (10 x L)/10000

= [10 (t_c -0.54) x 16.8] / 10000

The values of L and area A for different values of time of concentration are calculated using above relationships. These are given in table 5.8.

Table 5.8 Values of flow distance in drain 'L' and catchment area 'A' for different values of Time of concentration

t_c (mts)	10	15	20	30	40	50	60	90	120
L (m)	159	243	327	495	663	831	999	1503	2007
A (hect)	0.159	0.243	0.327	0.495	0.663	0.831	0.999	1.503	2.007

For the given case of SH-14 the value of L is 500 m, which gives a concentration time of about 30 minutes. Further design, therefore, is checked based upon the concentration time of 30 minutes.

5.4.3   Determination of Design Discharge

Discharge as given by eq. (2.3), Q	= 0.028 PAIc cum/sec
Coefficient of Runoff, P (table 2.3, Fig. 5.4)	= $(0.9 \times 4.5 + 0.3 \times 5.5)/(4.5 + 5.5) = 0.57$
Area of catchment, A	= 10x500/10000 = 0.5 hect

For t_c = 30 min, critical intensity of rainfall from table 4.4, Ic

$$= 6.01 \text{ cm/hr}$$

Therefore, Q (for 2 yr frequency)	= $0.028 \times 0.57 \times 0.5 \times 6.01$ = 0.048 cum/sec
Q for 25 yr frequency (table 4.3)	= 0.048 x 2.22 = 0.106 cum/sec

Adding 25% for discharge from intermediate drains, design discharge Q

for 02 yr frequency	= 0.048 x 1.25 = 0.06 cum/sec
for 25 yr frequency	= 0.106 x 1.25 = 0.133 cum/sec

5.4.4   Drain Section Calculations

Assume a rectangular drain x-section of 60 cm (width) x 30 cm (depth)

Free board	= 15 cm (from table 2.6)
Depth of flow	= 30-15 = 15 cm
Area of cross section of flow, A	= 0.6 x 0.15 = 0.09 m²
Wetted perimeter, p	= 0.6+0.15+0.15 = 0.9 m
Hydraulic mean radius, R=A/p	= 0.1 m
Gradient of drain bed, S	= 1 in 750

Manning's 'n' value (for plastered brick surface, table 2.4)

$$= 0.015$$

As per eq. (2.4), mean velocity, V	$= V = (1/n)\, R^{2/3}\, S^{1/2} = 0.524 \text{m/sec}$ (OK as per table 2.5)

Discharge, Q from eq. (2.5) $= A \times V = 0.09 \times 0.524 = 0.047$ cum/sec, which is less than 0.06, hence not OK.

Actual drain size already provided $= 0.6$ m x 0.3 m.
This size is not OK even for 2 yr storm frequency discharge.

Assume another trial section of 60 cm (width) x 35 cm (depth)

Free board $= 15$ cm (from table 2.6)

Depth of flow $= 35\text{-}15 = 20$ cm

Area of cross section of flow, A $= 0.6 \times 0.2 = 0.12$ m²

Wetted perimeter, p $= 0.6+0.2+0.2 = 1.0$ m

Hydraulic mean radius, R=A/p $= 0.12$ m

Gradient of drain bed, S $= 1$ in 750

Manning's 'n' value (for plastered brick surface, table 2.4)
   $= 0.015$

As per eq. (2.4), mean velocity, V $= V = (1/n) R^{2/3} S^{1/2} = 0.592$ m/sec
   (OK as per table 2.5)

Discharge, Q from eq. (2.5) $= A \times V = 0.12 \times 0.592 = 0.071$ cum/sec, which is more than than 0.06 cum/sec

Therefore, for storm frequency of 2 years, a minimum section of 0.6 m x 0.35m would be adequate.

Assume another trial section of 60 cm (width) x 50 cm (depth)

Free board $= 15$ cm (from table 2.6)

Depth of flow $= 50\text{-}15 = 35$ cm

Area of cross section of flow, A $= 0.6 \times 0.35 = 0.21$ m²

Wetted perimeter, p $= 0.6+0.35+0.35 = 1.3$ m

Hydraulic mean radius, R=A/p $= 0.162$ m

Gradient of drain bed, S $= 1$ in 750

Manning's 'n' value (for plastered brick surface, table 2.4)
   $= 0.015$

As per eq. (2.4), mean velocity, V	$=V=(1/n)\,R^{2/3}\,S^{1/2}=0.722\,m/sec$ (OK as per table 2.5)
Discharge, Q from eq. (2.5)	$= A \times V = 0.21\times0.722 = 0.152$ cum/sec, which is more than than 0.133 cum/sec

Therefore, for storm frequency of 25 years, a minimum section of 0.6 m x 0.5 m would be adequate.

5.5 DESIGN OF ROAD DRAIN FOR PANIPAT SANOLI ROAD, SH-16

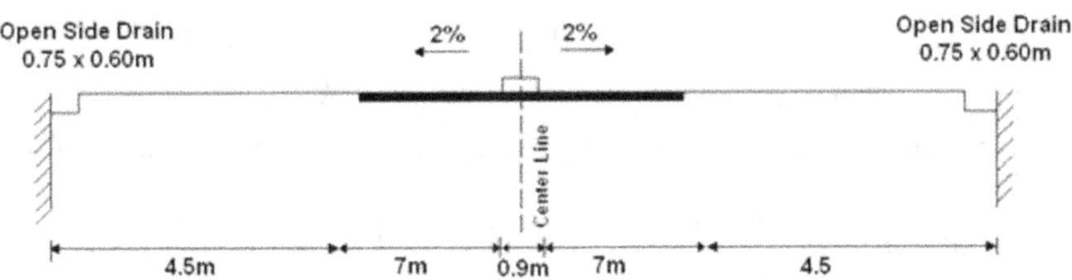

Fig. 5.5 Cross section of SH-16, Panipat Sanoli Road

5.5.1 Given Data of Road and Road Side Drain

Slope of bituminous surface	= 0.02 (equal to camber)
Width of paved surface (fig. 5.5)	= 7.0 m
Width of shoulder (fig. 5.5)	= 4.5 m (includes adjoining land)
Spacing of kerb inlets	= No kerbs
Gradient in the kerb channel	= NA
Size of road side drain provided	= 0.75 m x 0.6 m (rectangular)
Slope of drain bed	= 1 in 925
Length of road side drain up to cross drainage	= 500 m

5.5.2 Calculation of Time of Concentration and Critical Rainfall Intensity

Time of concentration has been calculated in a similar manner as discussed in section 5.2. It is given in table 5.9.

Table 5.9 Time of Concentration for SH-16

Section	Direction of Flow	L (km)	H (m)	t_1 (hrs)	t_2 (hrs)	t_3 (hrs)	t_c (hrs)	Speed (m/s)
Road surface	Transverse	0.0124	0.248	0.01	-	-	-	0.34
Kerb channel	Longitudinal	-	-	-	-	-	-	-
Drain	Longitudinal	0.5	0.54			0.54	-	0.26
Time of concentration t_c (hrs) = t_1 + t_2 + t_3 =							0.6 hr =36 mts	

Average speed of water on road $\quad$ =12.4 / (0.01 x 3600)=0.34 m/sec

Speed of water in drain $\quad$ = 500/(0.54x 3600) = 0.26 m/sec

Alternatively, time of concentration can be calculated by speed of water also

t_c (minutes) $\quad$ = (12.4/0.34)x1/60 + L/(0.26x60)

$\quad$ = 0.61 + (L /15.6)

L (flow distance in drain, metres) $\quad$ = (t_c -0.61) x 15.6

A (Area contributing to flow upto L m in hect)

$\quad$ = (12.4 x L)/10000

$\quad$ = [12.4 (t_c -0.61) x 15.6] / 10000

The values of L and area A for different values of time of concentration are calculated using above relationships. These are given in table 5.10.

Table 5.10 Values of flow distance in drain 'L' and catchment area 'A' for different values of Time of concentration

t_c (mts)	10	15	20	30	40	50	60	90	120
L (m)	146	224	302	458	614	770	926	1394	1862
A (hect)	0.182	0.278	0.375	0.569	0.762	0.955	1.149	1.729	2.309

For the given case of SH-16, the value of L is 500 m which gives a concentration time of about 33 minutes. Further design is, however, checked based upon the concentration time of 30 minutes only keeping in view the fact that shoulders are provided with more cross slope than camber on the pavement which will result in more speed of water and lesser concentration time.

5.5.3 Determination of Design Discharge

Discharge as given by eq. (2.3), Q	= 0.028 PAIc cum/sec
Coefficient of Runoff, P (table 2.3, Fig. 5.5)	= $(0.9\times7.9+0.3\times4.5)/(7.9+4.5)=0.68$
Area of catchment, A	= $12.4\times500/10000 = 0.62$ hect

For t_c = 30 min, critical intensity of rainfall from table 5.4, Ic

$$= 6.01 \text{ cm/hr}$$

Therefore, Q (for 2 yr frequency)	= $0.028\times0.68\times0.62\times6.01=0.071$ cum/sec
Q for 25 yr frequency (table 5.3)	= $0.071 \times 2.22 = 0.158$ cum/sec

Adding 25% for discharge from intermediate drains, design discharge Q

for 02 yr frequency	= $0.071 \times 1.25 = 0.089$ cum/sec
for 25 yr frequency	= $0.158 \times 1.25 = 0.198$ cum/sec

5.5.4 Drain Section Calculations

Assume a rectangular drain x-section of 60 cm (width) x 45 cm (depth)

Free board	= 15 cm (from table 2.6)
Depth of flow	= 45-15 = 30 cm
Area of cross section of flow, A	= $0.6 \times 0.3 = 0.18$ m²
Wetted perimeter, p	= 0.6+0.3+0.3 = 1.2 m
Hydraulic mean radius, R=A/p	= 0.15 m
Gradient of drain bed, S	= 1 in 925

Manning's 'n' value (for plastered brick surface, table 2.4)

$$= 0.015$$

As per eq. (2.4), mean velocity, V	$=V=(1/n)R^{2/3}S^{1/2}=0.619$ m/sec (OK as per table 2.5)
Discharge, Q from eq. (2.5)	= $A \times V = 0.18\times0.619 = 0.111$

cum/sec, which is more than 0.089, hence OK for 2 yr frequency design discharge.

Assume another trial section of 75 cm (width) x 55 cm (depth)

Free board	= 15 cm (from table 2.6)
Depth of flow	= 55-15 = 40 cm
Area of cross section of flow, A	= 0.75 x 0.4 = 0.3 m²
Wetted perimeter, p	= 0.75+0.4+0.4 = 1.55 m
Hydraulic mean radius, R=A/p	= 0.194 m
Gradient of drain bed, S	= 1 in 925
Manning's 'n' value (for plastered brick surface, table 2.4)	= 0.015
As per eq. (2.4), mean velocity, V	$= V=(1/n) R^{2/3} S^{1/2}= 0.733$ m/sec (OK as per table 2.5)
Discharge, Q from eq. (2.5)	= A x V = 0.3x0.733 = 0.22 cum/sec, which is more than than 0.198cum/sec

Therefore, for storm frequency of 25 years, a minimum section of 0.75m x 0.55 m would be adequate

Actual drain size already provided	= 0.75 m x 0.60 m. This is adequate for 25 yr frequency storm discharge.

5.6 RELATIONSHIPS BETWEEN DESIGN PARAMETERS

5.6.1 Relationship between Time of Concentration (t_c) and Flow Length of Drain (L)

Values of flow length of drain 'L' for different values of time of concentration 't_c' for the four roads selected for the study are given tables 5.2, 5.6, 5.8 and 5.10 respectively. The data from these tables have been used to develop mathematical relationships between time of concentration and flow length. These relationships have been developed using excel package of M.S. Office and are shown in Fig. 5.6 to 5.9. These relationships are also summarized in table 5.11. It is observed from these relationships that width of carriageway, adjoining shoulders, cross slope of the road and bed slope of the drain have a little influence over the time of concentration which mainly depends upon length of flow of water in the drain. Therefore, a simplified general relationship valid for all roads can be deduced from the given relationships for the four number roads studied in this research work. This general relationship is also given in table 5.11.

Table 5.11 Relationship between Time of Concentration (t_c) and Flow Length of Drain (L)

Name of Road	Width of Carriage-way contribu-ting towards flow in side drain (m)	Total width of area contribu-ting towards flow in side drain (m)	Dist-ance bet-ween kerb inlets (m)	Cross slope of road %	Longi-tu-dinal slope of drain bed	Relation-ship	*R^2
NH-1	20	24	30	2.5	1 in 675	$t_c = 0.0617$ L+2.284	1
NH-71A	4.5	19	-	1.5	1 in 675	$t_c = 0.0575$ L+0.977	1
SH-14	4.5	10	-	2.0	1 in 750	$t_c = 0.0595$ L+0.536	1
SH-16	7.0	12.4	-	2.0	1 in 925	$t_c = 0.0641$ L+0.641	1
General relationship valid for all roads that can be deduced from above relationships for these four roads						$t_c = 0.06$ L t_c in mts, L in m	

* R^2 is co-efficient of determination

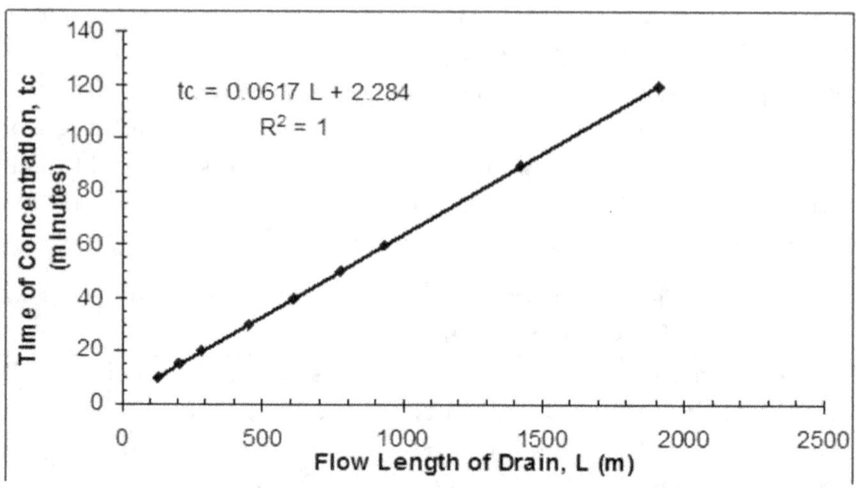

Fig. 5.6 Relationship between Time of Concentration and Flow Length of Drain for NH-1

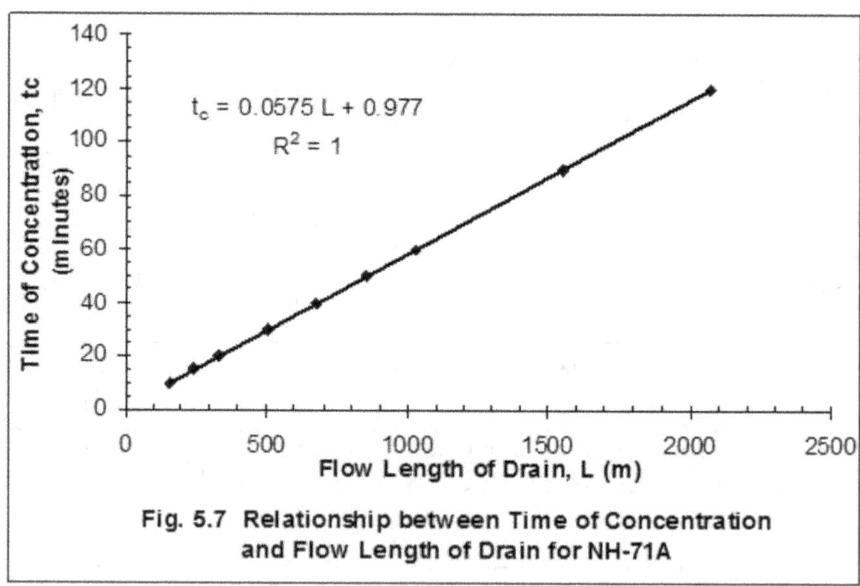

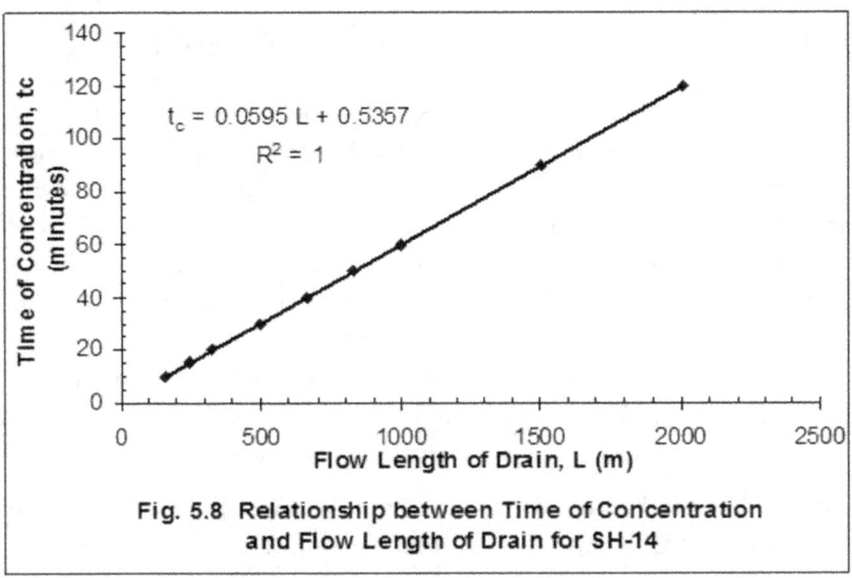

Fig. 5.8 Relationship between Time of Concentration and Flow Length of Drain for SH-14

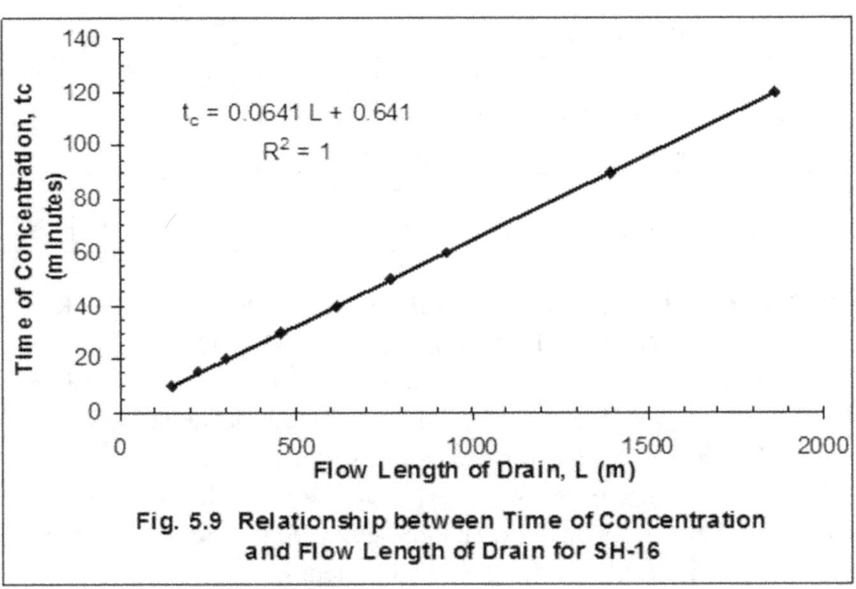

Fig. 5.9 Relationship between Time of Concentration and Flow Length of Drain for SH-16

5.6.2 Relationship between Critical Intensity of Rainfall (Ic) and Time of Concentration (t_c)

Rainfall intensity values for different durations of rainfall for a storm frequency (return period) of 2 years is given in table 5.4. The data from this table have been used to develop mathematical relationship between intensity of rainfall (Ic) and time of concentration (t_c). Similarly, the data from table 5.3 have been used to develop mathematical relationship between conversion factor 'F' (with respect to 02 years return period of storm) and any return period 'T' of the storm. These relationships have been developed using excel package of M.S. Office and are shown in Fig. 5.10 and 5.11. The relationships are also given in table 5.12.

Table 5.12 Relationships between Critical Intensity of Rainfall and Time of Concentration, and conversion factor

Design parameters	Relationship	R^2
Intensity of rainfall Ic (in cm/hr) for 02 yr return period of storm and time of concentration t_c in minutes	$Ic = 36.499\ t_c^{-0.5539}$	0.9869
Conversion factor F (wrt 02 yr return period) for determining intensity of rainfall for design return period T (in yrs)	$F = 0.8868\ T^{0.2817}$	0.9695
Intensity of rainfall Ic (in cm/hr) for T yr design return period of storm	$Ic = F \times 36.5\ t_c^{-0.55}$	–

5.7 PROCEDURAL APPLICATION OF RESEARCH FOR DETERMINATION OF DESIGN DISCHARGE

From the forgoing analyses of the results of the study, the procedure for determining design discharge for design of roadside drainage system is summarized in the following steps for its easy application.

1. Determine length of flow of water in the drain (L), which would be the length between the inlet point and the next intercepting cross drain, or between two consecutive intercepting cross drains.

2. Calculate time of concentration 't_c' using the following equation as obtained from table 5.11.

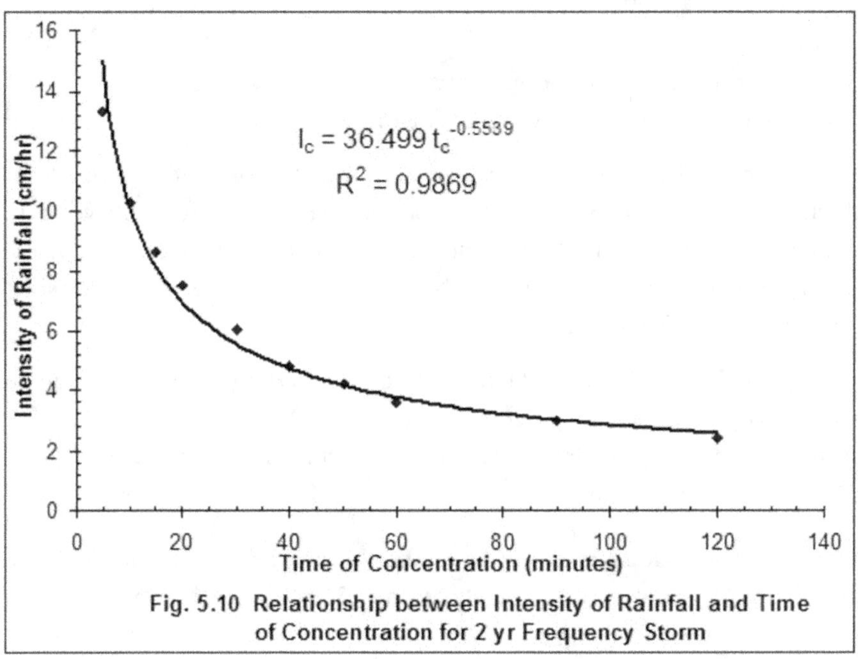

Fig. 5.10 Relationship between Intensity of Rainfall and Time of Concentration for 2 yr Frequency Storm

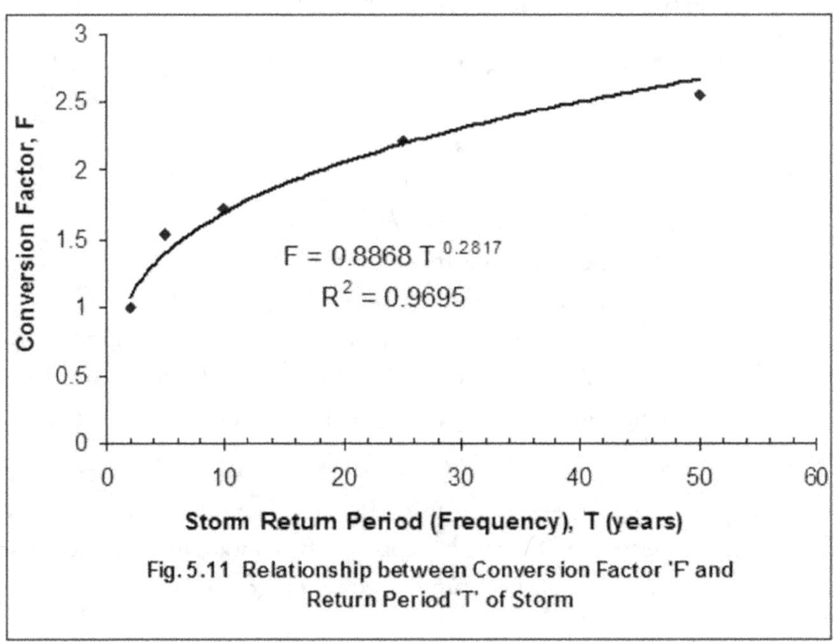

Fig. 5.11 Relationship between Conversion Factor 'F and Return Period 'T' of Storm

$$t_c = 0.06 \, L \tag{5.1}$$

where

t_c = time of concentration in minutes

L = Length of flow of water in the drain in metres

3. Decide the design return period of storm for determining design discharge for the drain. The return period may be taken as 02 years for minor roads / roads of less importance whereas it can be taken as 25 years for higher category roads such as NH and SH. For road of intermediate importance, it cab taken as 05 to 10 years.

4. Calculate conversion factor 'F' for converting critical intensity of rainfall for 02 years return period of storm to the design return period of storm 'T' years using equation (5.2) as obtained from table 5.12.

$$F = 0.89 \, T^{0.28} \tag{5.2}$$

5. Find out critical intensity of rainfall Ic (cm/hr) for the design return period of T years of storm using equation (5.3) as obtained from table 5.12.

$$Ic = F \times 36.5 \, t_c^{-0.55} \tag{5.3}$$

where

t_c = time of concentration in minutes given by eq. 5.1.

6. Calculate design discharge using rational formula given in following equation

$$Q = (0.028 \, PAIc) \times C_b \tag{5.4}$$

where

Q = design discharge in cum/sec

P = coefficient of Runoff obtained from table 2.3

A = area of catchment in hect.

   = (width of carriageway and adjoing land contributing to flow in side drain in m x flow length of drain 'L' in m)/10000

I_c = critical intensity of rainfall in cm/hr given by eq. (5.3)

C_b = correction factor varying from 1 to 2 which takes care of additional discharge coming into the drain from intermediate small drains and also of reduction in capacity of the drain likely to be caused by partial blockage of the drain due to several reasons.

6 DRAINAGE ISSUES AND SUGGESTED DESIGN IMPROVEMENTS

6.1 DRAINAGE ISSUES

The road drainage issues with which most of the cities and towns in countries like India are facing today have been identified with the help of a study undertaken in Panipat city. The main issues related to poor drainage of roads are identified as:

(i)   The storm water of the city flows through Panipat drain (Gandha Nala). This drain also acts as the carrier of polluted effluent of industries and the treated effluent of city sewage. The surface run-off from roads is collected along the roadside through storm water drains and is discharged through cross drainage works in the Panipat drain.

(ii)   The city does not have a systematic solid waste disposal system with the collected garbage being dumped in the low lying areas of the city, usually near the railway lines and the vacant low lying plots.

(iii) Drainage system of Panipat city suffers from the problems of silting of drains, non-integration of various drains, absence of connectivity between the drains, blocked water way near culverts, blockages by various types of solid wastes and mixing of polluted effluents of industry and sewage into the storm water. Lack of regular cleaning and maintenance of drains also leads to poor drainage conditions in the city.

(iv)   The road side drains on most of the roads are located beneath the approach passage of adjoining shops with intervening ground between roads and drain having adverse slope towards the road. This makes the drains redundant, which are invariably used as dumping places for garbage of the shops.

The roads like NH-1 having the side drains located by the side of edge of road pavement away from beneath the passage of shops are observed to have better road drainage.

(v)   Due to absence of any sewerage system in almost half the city area, the road side open drains receive all sullage water, over flow from septic tanks and soakage pits, and raw sewage along the NH-1 and other roads. This ultimately gets discharged into River Yamuna through Panipat drain and main drain causing contamination of water and health hazards.

(vi)   The water on both sides of most of the culverts remains stagnant due to blocked waterways, which results in poor sanitary conditions and breeding of mosquitoes etc.

6.2 DESIGN ISSUES

The adequacies / inadequacies of the design of the road side drainage system have been worked out for the city undertaken in the study. These are:

(i)   The roadside drainage system for all the four main roads of the city selected for this study has been designed. It is observed that the existing drain size of 1.0 m x 1.0 m for NH-1 (Delhi-Ambala Road) is adequate for road drainage. The drain size required for 02 years and 25 years frequency design discharge is found to be 0.6 m x 0.50 m and 1.0 m x 0.55 m respectively.

(ii)   For NH-71A (Panipat Gohana Road), the existing drain size of 0.6 m x 0.4 m is found to be inadequate for 25 years frequency design discharge. The drain size should be 0.6 m x 0.6 m to meet this requirement.

(iii)   For SH-14 (Panipat Assandh Road), the existing drain size of 0.6 m x 0.3 m is found to be inadequate even for 02 years frequency design discharge. The drain size should be 0.6 m x 0.35 m and 0.6 m x 0.5 m to meet the requirement of 02 years and 25 year frequency design discharge respectively.

(iv)   For SH-16 (Panipat Meerut Road / Sanoli Road), the existing drain size of 0.75 m x 0.6 m is found to be adequate for road drainage. The drain size should be 0.6 m x 0.45 m and 0.75 m x 0.55 m to meet the requirement of 02 years and 25 year frequency design discharge respectively.

(v)   The design of roadside drainage system in respect of the studied roads indicates that the size of existing drains is provided arbitrarily without having any uniform design criteria for the design of roadside drainage.

6.3   SUGGESTED DESIGN IMPROVEMENTS

As the existing guidelines for the design of road side drainage system have some shortcomings in respect of clarity on some of the design parameters and their complexity to use. These issues have been tried to address with simplified easy to use guidelines which have their main points as:

(i)   Mathematical relationships have been developed between various parameters to determine the design discharge in an easy manner.

(ii)   It is observed from the study that width of carriageway, adjoining shoulders, cross slope of the road and bed slope of the drain have a little influence over the time of concentration which mainly depends upon length of flow of water in the drain. Keeping this fact into consideration, a very simple relation between time of concentration 'tc' and length of flow of water in the drain 'L' has been suggested in the form

$$t_c = 0.06 \, L$$

(iii)   Similarly, an equation has been suggested to calculate conversion factor 'F' for converting critical intensity of rainfall for 02 years return period of storm to the design return period of storm 'T' years which is given as

$$F = 0.89 \, T^{0.28}$$

(iv)   A relationship to find out critical intensity of rainfall Ic for the design return period of 'T' years of storm has also been developed as

$$Ic = F \times 36.5 \, t_c^{-0.55}$$

(v)   The relevant IRC standards for the design of road drainage [1,2,6] do not clearly specify the return period or frequency of storm to be adopted for different category of roads for determining the design discharge. Similarly, the procedure for determining the design discharge is also not given in a simplified manner by these codes.

(vi)   Guidelines have been given in the study for adopting appropriate return period of storm for determining design discharge for different category of roads.

(vii) A simplified stepwise procedure is evolved in the study for determining design discharge for the design of roadside drainage. system for roads.

REFERENCES

1. Indian Roads Congress (IRC:SP:50, 1999), *Guidelines on Urban Drainage*, New Delhi.

2. Indian Roads Congress (IRC:SP:13, 2004), *Guidelines for the Design of Small Bridges and Culverts*, New Delhi.

3. MORTH (Ministry of Road Transport and Highways) (IV Revision, 2001), *Specifications for Road and Bridge Works*, Indian Roads Congress, New Delhi.

4. *Open Series Topographic Map No. 53 C/13*, Survey of India, 2007, Dehradun

5. *Soil Testing Reports* (2005-09), Highway Engineering Lab, NIT Kurukshetra

6. Kimmel TM (2000) *"Weather and Climate : Koppen climate classification flow chart"* University of Texas at Austin. Retrieved 2007 – 04 -08

7. http://maps.Gov.in./*Average Rainfall in Haryana*, Survey of India,2005,Dehradun

8. Indian Roads Congress (IRC:SP:42, 1994), *Guidelines on Road Drainage*, New Delhi.

www.ingramcontent.com/pod-product-compliance
Lightning Source LLC
Chambersburg PA
CBHW061720250726
48657CB00002B/689